No more Mr. N

By- Gaurav

Table of Contents

Disclaimer:

This is a work of fiction. Names, characters, places, events, and incidents mentioned in this book are the product of the author's imagination or used in a fictitious manner. Any resemblance to actual persons, living or dead, or actual events is purely coincidental.

The views, thoughts, and opinions expressed by the characters in this book do not necessarily reflect those of the author or publisher. The author does not intend to offend any individual, group, or community.

Although efforts have been made to ensure the accuracy and reliability of the information presented in this book, the author and the publisher do not assume any responsibility or liability for errors or omissions.

Reading this book is at your own risk. The author and publisher shall not be held responsible for any loss or damage arising from the use of this book.

About the Author

Gaurav Garg is an internationally accomplished marketing leader, author, and speaker. He holds an MBA focused on marketing strategy and has over 20 years of experience driving growth, innovation, and customer engagement for leading global brands.

Gaurav has authored numerous books across a diverse range of topics, including psychology, personal growth, wellness, spirituality, and business strategy. His works have garnered praise for their practical wisdom, research-backed frameworks, and transformative insights presented in an accessible style.

A few of Gaurav's most popular titles include:

- Unlocking the Mind: How Behaviour Reveals Personality
- The Don's Reckoning
- Corporate Warriors: Applying Chanaky's Arthashastra in Business
- Young Titans – Teach your kids to be mentally strong
- Mental Mastery: Brain Exercises for Continuous Development
- Harnessing Circadian Rhythms for an Optimal Life
- Analysing Your Dog's Personality: A Roadmap to a Deeper Bond
- Karma's Role in Our Conscience: From Angel to Demon and Back Again
- The Art of Positivity: Mastering Your Mindset for a Better Life
- The Illusion of Perception: How Our Mind Trick Us

- 100 Ayurvedic Herbs for Health and Fitness: Unlocking Nature's Healing Secrets
- The Bhagwad Geeta: Ancient Wisdom for Modern Life
- Breaking the Darkness: A Journey Through Depression
- Navigating Corporate Politics: A Roadmap for Success
- 25 approach frameworks with examples for writing effective Business mails
- The Bull's guide to life: Understanding Taurus traits and characteristics .

Gaurav is passionate about synthesizing ancient wisdom and modern science into practical guidance that helps individuals and organizations reach their full potential.

Website: askwebman.com

Email: gauravrgarg@gmail.com

DEDICATION

Dedicated to my father, Shri R.S. GARG

My father has been my greatest teacher and inspiration. As an esteemed educator who served as-

Vice Principal-The Scindia School, Gwalior

Founding Principal- Gokuldas Public School, Khargone

He has devoted his life to imparting knowledge and wisdom to thousands.

His unwavering support encourages me daily to pursue my passions to the fullest. He exemplifies the values of diligence, dedication, and perseverance that fuel my drive. Without his guidance, I would not be where I am today.

This book stands as a testament to his immeasurable influence on my life. I am forever grateful for the gift of his timeless teachings and for the countless lives he has enriched through his leadership.

Author's Preface

Assertiveness is one of the most valuable skills anyone can cultivate, yet also one of the most challenging. After a lifetime of cultural conditioning toward compliance and conflict avoidance, embracing assertive communication requires transformative personal growth. It takes courage to find your voice after being silenced.

My aim in writing this book is to provide guidance and encouragement for that journey based on both professional expertise and personal experience. I spent over a decade passive and afraid to advocate for myself. People-pleasing and swallowing negative emotions took immense psychological effort - not to mention enabling others to take advantage of me.

Eventually I reached a breaking point and committed to change. Through researching assertiveness skills, practicing them even when uncomfortable, and immersing myself in personal development, I slowly transformed my communication tendencies. The more I asserted my boundaries, expressed my needs, and claimed my worth, the more empowered I felt. It significantly improved my confidence, relationships, and career.

Of course no one masters assertiveness overnight. It's a lifelong process, and I still stumble on occasion. But the overall trajectory has been transformative. My only regret is not embarking on the assertiveness journey sooner.

It is my hope this book will shorten your learning curve. The pages ahead provide actionable steps for building assertiveness tailored to your specific challenges and personality. You'll learn how to navigate difficult conversations, confront manipulative behavior, break lifelong passive habits, overcome self-doubt and much more.

Each chapter includes examples across both personal and professional contexts for diverse situations. No matter what assertiveness dilemmas you face, you will find applicable guidance within these pages.

Most importantly, this book will remind you that becoming assertive is not about fixing yourself, but honoring and unleashing your true self. You deserve - and absolutely can - find your voice.

Chapter 1: Introduction

Do you feel you often get taken advantage of and have difficulty standing up for yourself? Do you struggle to say "no" when someone asks a favor, even if you don't have the time or resources? Do you frequently set aside your own needs and priorities to avoid conflict?

If so, you're not alone. Many people, regardless of gender, struggle with being too passive and reluctant to advocate for their wants.

This tendency stems from social conditioning beginning in childhood. As kids, we're taught to "be nice," obey authority figures, and put others' needs first. Qualities like assertiveness and ego are discouraged.

Later as adults, we fear appearing too bold or opinionated will lead to social or professional consequences. We opt to keep the peace rather than make waves.

This pattern leads many to chronically suppress their own preferences and swallow dissatisfaction to please others. They have trouble setting boundaries, worrying about backlash. They politely go with the flow rather than asking for what they want.

But consistently prioritizing others' needs before your own damages self-esteem and breeds resentment. Failing to self-advocate also enables others to exploit you. You may struggle to achieve professional goals requiring assertiveness like seeking promotions. Too much passivity likewise harms relationships through unhealthy dynamics.

The good news is developing greater assertiveness is possible with intention. You can learn to confidently stand up for yourself, communicate wants and opinions, set boundaries, and stop being a pushover.

True assertiveness involves advocating for your legitimate rights while respecting others' rights too. It requires clear communication, empathy, control, and fairness. The aim is not to become aggressive or steamroll people.

This book will teach you to become more assertive in all facets of life. You'll learn to overcome fears, set boundaries, speak up about grievances, and prioritize your needs.

Let's look at examples of how lacking assertiveness frequently hinders people:

Example 1: Unable to Say No at Work

James is an analyst at a financial firm. He takes pride in consistently going above-and-beyond for colleagues who need help. But James often overcommits because he can't say no when asked for favors.

This leaves James stretched thin, stressed, and working long hours to deliver on promises. His inability to set boundaries starts impacting his health and relationship outside work.

To be more assertive, James needs to get comfortable declining colleagues when he is at capacity:

"I'm slammed this week and can't take on anything more right now. Perhaps I could help you next week once this project is wrapped up?"

This politely conveys his limits without confrontation. Over time, James must keep enforcing boundaries so colleagues don't take advantage.

Example 2: Unable to Enforce Expectations in Relationships

Salma has been clear with her new boyfriend Nate that she needs a lot of quality time together in a relationship to feel secure. But after a few months, Nate's busy schedule leads him to cancel several dates in a row.

Salma feels hurt but avoids confronting Nate to sidestep potential conflict. Her resentment silently builds even though she won't stand up for her clearly communicated need.

To be assertive, Salma can tactfully reinforce her expectation:

"Nate, I've told you I need consistency in seeing each other to feel secure. I care about you, but if that doesn't work for you, this won't be the right relationship for me."

This lets Salma assert her needs without aggression. If Nate still ignores them, she can walk away knowing she stood up for herself.

Example 3: Acquiescing Instead of Voicing Your Opinion

At family dinners, Mason's uncle often expresses polarizing political views. Mason feels uncomfortable but bites his tongue to keep the peace, even when he strongly disagrees.

An assertive approach would involve Mason tactfully providing his perspective:

"I have a very different viewpoint, but I'm happy to discuss our differences respectfully. There's value in being open to diverse opinions."

This allows Mason to voice his thoughts while minimizing unnecessary conflict. If his uncle won't engage in thoughtful debate, Mason may need to avoid certain topics.

Example 4: Downplaying Your Qualifications

Sarah has 5 years of managing her department successfully, but is hesitant to apply when a Director role opens up. She worries she'll seem arrogant pursuing such a big promotion.

Rather than downplaying herself, Sarah can confidently but tactfully advocate for the role:

"Based on exceeding goals and taking on leadership responsibilities these past 5 years, I believe I've shown I'm ready to step into a Director role. I'm very interested in the opportunity."

This highlights her qualifications instead of diminishing them. Self-advocacy is key to advancement.

Example 5: Tolerating Disrespectful Comments

At a networking mixer, Alex is asked what he does for work. When he shares his role, a woman responds: *"My husband would never let me work outside the home."*

Though very offensive, Alex simply smiles politely to avoid an awkward situation. Later, he wishes he'd stood up for himself.

Alex could have responded assertively but calmly:

"I don't share those views on women in the workplace. I hope we can still have a respectful discussion."

This lets Alex voice his disagreement without escalating conflict. Assertiveness means standing up for yourself graciously.

As these examples illustrate, assertiveness empowers people of all genders to confront challenging situations. This book will equip you to become more assertive in every area by teaching you how to:

- Establish and enforce healthy boundaries
- Confidently communicate your needs and opinions
- Recognize manipulative or passive-aggressive behavior
- Say "no" instead of always acquiescing
- Stand up to bullying, sexism, racism, and other toxic behaviors
- Pursue advancement and leadership opportunities
- Resolve conflicts through tactful discussion
- Maintain positive relationships built on mutual respect
- And more!

Building new assertive habits takes moving past deeply rooted fears and cultural conditioning. It can initially feel uncomfortable. But with practice, asserting yourself becomes second nature.

The rewards extend far beyond increased confidence and inner strength. Becoming more assertive inspires those around you to also stand up for themselves. Each small act chips away at double standards and oppression.

Are you ready to stop putting other people first and start prioritizing your wants? Will you challenge lifelong people-pleasing habits and find your voice? If so, let's begin building your assertiveness foundation.

Chapter 2: Understanding Assertiveness

In Chapter 1, we explored why lack of assertiveness holds many people back and looked at examples across different contexts. Now let's dive deeper into what exactly assertiveness means.

What is Assertiveness?

Assertiveness is the ability to confidently stand up for yourself and your rights while also respecting others. It involves clearly expressing your needs, wants, boundaries, and perspectives without being aggressive or diminishing other people.

Some key elements of assertiveness include:

● Direct communication: Speaking plainly and honestly about your needs and viewpoints.

● Confidence: Believing your desires and opinions have value and are worth voicing.

● Respect: Expressing yourself in ways that don't infringe on rights of others. Not being dismissive, rude or humiliating.

● Compromise: Willingness to find solutions that meet your needs while also considering others' perspective.

● Empathy: Understanding where others are coming from, even if you disagree with their viewpoint.

● Emotional control: Staying calm and thoughtful rather than escalating anger and aggressiveness.

● Fairness: Pursuing an outcome that is morally right and equitable, not just most convenient for you.

Assertiveness does not equate to aggressiveness or selfishness. The goal is not to dominate others, disregard their needs, or express yourself in hostile ways.

True assertiveness finds the balance between passively sacrificing your own needs and pursuing them through bullying. It allows you to healthily advocate for yourself while maintaining positive relationships built on mutual understanding.

Contrasting Passive, Aggressive, and Assertive Styles

To better understand what assertiveness looks like, it helps to contrast it with other communication styles:

Passive:

- Prioritizes pleasing others over your own wants/needs
- Avoids expressing thoughts, needs, and emotions
- Allows mistreatment/disrespect from others
- Frequently says "yes" when you want to say "no"
- Doesn't defend your boundaries
- Lowers/hesitates expressing your viewpoint
- Apologizes excessively Aggressive:
- Prioritizes own needs regardless of impact on others
- Dominates discussions, interrupts, ignores others' perspectives
- Hostile, confrontational, insulting tone
- Expresses opinions forcefully without empathy
- Invades others' boundaries/space
- Refuses compromise
- Issues threats/ultimatums to coerce outcomes Assertive
- Balances advocating for self while respecting others
- Clear, confident expression of your needs and viewpoint
- Calm, thoughtful tone focused on resolution
- Compromises when appropriate to be equitable
- Empathizes with others' perspectives
- Enforces boundaries while respecting others' rights
- Stands ground on values while finding mutual understanding

Assertiveness falls in the middle - not being a pushover but also not being a bully. It's about finding win-win solutions whenever possible through open and respectful communication.

Now let's look at some examples of how passive, aggressive, and assertive responses contrast in real-life situations:

Example 1 - At Work

Your boss unfairly blames you for a mistake you didn't make.

Passive response: Say nothing and accept blame, even though you don't deserve it, to keep the boss happy.

Aggressive response: Lash out at your boss, aggressively deny responsibility, and refuse to discuss it further.

Assertive response: Calmly explain you had no involvement in the mistake and provide evidence supporting your case. Suggest working together to prevent future misunderstandings.

Example 2 - In Friendships

A close friend frequently makes insensitive jokes about a sensitive issue you've asked them to stop.

Passive response: Force yourself to laugh along to avoid confrontation even though you're upset.

Aggressive response: Blow up at your friend, insult them, threaten to end the friendship unless they stop immediately.

Assertive response: Have a thoughtful discussion reiterating your boundary and explaining why the jokes are hurtful. Give them a chance to adjust behavior while enforcing consequences if they continue.

Example 3 - In Relationships

Your partner rarely wants to socialize with your friend group, but often pressures you to hang out with theirs.

Passive response: Always go along with what your partner wants and neglect your own social preferences to make them happy.

Aggressive response: Refuse to ever see your partner's friends again and demand they socialize with your group from now on instead.

Assertive response: Have an open conversation about taking turns and compromising on social plans so both your needs are met. If they won't compromise, limit the time you spend with people who don't support the relationship.

Example 4 - In Family Relationships

A family member makes a racist, homophobic or otherwise bigoted statement around you.

Passive response: Say nothing to avoid an argument, even though you feel very uncomfortable.

Aggressive response: Call them out in a hostile, aggressive way that escalates a big fight.

Assertive response: Calmly but firmly state you don't share those views and find them offensive. If needed, politely exit the situation.

Example 5 - In Public/Among Strangers

A stranger gropes you in a bar.

Passive response: Quietly move away and say nothing to avoid a confrontation.

Aggressive response: Loudly shout at them and violently shove them away from you.

Assertive response: Firmly tell them, "Don't touch me," and notify bar staff or authorities to handle the situation properly.

As you can see from these examples, assertiveness provides a balanced solution focused on defending your own boundaries while remaining thoughtful, empathetic and solution-oriented.

Now that you understand the principles of assertiveness, we'll move on to identifying your personal barriers to assertive behavior in Chapter 3.

Chapter 3: Identifying Your Barriers to Assertiveness

In the previous chapters, we explored the importance of assertiveness and differentiated it from passive and aggressive communication styles. Now let's examine some of the common barriers that prevent people from being assertive so you can recognize patterns in your own life.

Fear of Conflict

Many passive people grew up in households where anger and disagreement were forbidden. Conflict avoidance feels safer, so they reflexively shy away from asserting their needs if it risks igniting tension.

Signs this applies to you:

● You dread confrontation and will do anything to appease others to keep the peace.

● You prioritize smooth relationships over your own preferences.

● You struggle to say no because it might upset someone.

● Rather than discussing grievances, you bottle up resentment until you explode.

Example: *Michelle hates her apartment, but when her partner's lease is up, she doesn't advocate looking for a new place because she's scared of conflict over housing disagreements.*

Fear of Disapproval

Some people sacrifice their needs because they can't handle others' disapproval. They modify their behavior to earn validation and avoid rejection. This stems from lack of self-confidence and caring too much what people think.

Signs this applies to you:

● You constantly seek others' approval and affirmation.

● You avoid expressing opinions that might be unpopular.

● You feel crushed by even mild criticism or disagreement.

● You stay silent instead of standing up for yourself to avoid judgment.

Example: *Matt doesn't ask his boss for a raise even though he deserves one because he's terrified of potential rejection.*

Habit of Pleasing Others

Life experiences can program a strong reflex to please others, sometimes stemming from manipulative or unstable caregivers. People-pleasers do what's asked of them, often at their own expense.

Signs this applies to you:

- You feel guilty saying no and will always agree to requests.
- You instinctively put others' preferences and needs first.
- You over-apologize and are excessively accommodating.
- It's easier for you to meet others' needs than your own.

Example: *Natalie always lets friends choose the restaurant when they go out so they'll be happy, even if she doesn't like the food.*

Fear of Seeming Selfish

Many people worry asserting their needs and boundaries will seem selfish, especially women who face stereotypes about being accommodating. They'd rather suffer in silence than speak up.

Signs this applies to you:

- You think prioritizing your well-being over others' needs is wrong.
- You downplay your own preferences and live reactively to others' wants.
- You're uncomfortable receiving gifts, favors or any gestures just for you.
- You feel too guilty to ever ask for help.

Example: *Lauren wants to plan a big trip for her 40th birthday but feels too guilty about taking time and money just for herself.*

Lack of Self-Confidence

It's difficult to advocate for your needs if you don't believe you deserve to have them met. You might rationalize mistreatment, make excuses for others, or feel your desires aren't important enough to bother anyone with.

Signs this applies to you:

- You frequently minimize your own needs, wants, and feelings.
- You assume others' priorities are more important than yours.
- You crave validation from others to make up for lack of self-worth.
- You are highly self-critical and think you don't deserve better.

Example: *James never speaks up about his workload because he figures colleagues' time must be more valuable.*

Fear of Losing Relationships

Some people with dependency issues tolerate poor treatment from others because they can't bear the idea of losing connections, even toxic ones. Their sense of security comes from relationships at any cost.

Signs this applies to you:

- You'd rather stay in an unhealthy relationship than be alone.
- Your social life revolves around pleasing difficult people.
- You believe mistreatment is better than no relationship at all.
- You will tolerate anything to "keep the peace" with family.

Example: *Gloria caters to her sister's unreasonable demands because she's terrified of damaging their lifelong bond.*

Perfectionism

Perfectionists avoid healthy conflict because they think they should already know how to handle every situation properly. Admitting ignorance or uncertainty feels like failure, so they say nothing rather than speak up about problems.

Signs this applies to you:

- You get paralyzed by fear of saying/doing the wrong thing.
- You'd rather tolerate mistreatment than handle confrontation "imperfectly".
- You are intensely self-critical when you don't handle situations "right."
- You avoid trying new things if you aren't already great at them.

Example: *Mark struggles to set any boundaries with his overbearing mother because he feels too anxious about messing it up.*

Do any of these mental barriers resonate with you? Most people experience a blend of factors inhibiting their assertiveness. Recognizing the patterns holding you back is the first step toward breaking them.

Now let's look at actionable strategies for overcoming these obstacles...

Helpful Strategies

For conflict avoidance:

- Remind yourself that healthy relationships require some constructive conflict. Avoiding tough conversations damages trust and intimacy.
- Start small by asserting yourself in low-stakes situations first to build confidence in your ability to handle disagreement.
- When confronting conflict, focus the discussion on resolution rather than blame. Frame it as you and the other person vs. the problem.

For fear of disapproval:

- Work on building your self-confidence and sense of value apart from others' validation. What do you admire about yourself?
- Journal about your deeper fears around rejection to develop more self-compassion. Recognize disapproval is unavoidable and your worth isn't defined by others.
- Remind yourself you can't control how people respond, you can only control whether you advocate for your needs.

For people-pleasing habits:

- Ask yourself if people-pleasing patterns stem from childhood experiences you've outgrown. How might asserting yourself more create healthier dynamics?
- Experiment with small moments of independence from the constant consideration of others' needs. Notice how doing something just for you feels.
- Journal about whether people-pleasing has led to resentment, enabled poor treatment from others, or harmed your self-identity.

For fear of selfishness:

- Admit you do have needs and you matter too - this isn't selfish, it's healthy self-care.

- Prioritize taking care of yourself first so you have the bandwidth to be present for others without burning out. You can't pour from an empty cup.
- Set boundaries around time/energy spent on others' demands to reserve space for your own self-care. Enforce them.

For lack of confidence:

- Make a list of your positive qualities and things you're proud of about yourself as a reminder of your value. Re-read it when you're feeling insecure.
- Journal about where under-confidence comes from. Were you criticized as a child or taught not to speak up? Challenge negative self-talk.
- Before asking for something, visualize the best-case scenario. Often people are more supportive than you expect. Think through potential positive outcomes.

For fear of loss:

- Remind yourself that no one deserves to be treated poorly, even if it means letting go of an unhealthy connection. You deserve meaningful relationships.
- Strengthen bonds with supportive people in your life who reaffirm your worth. Build a sense of security internally rather than through difficult people.
- Envision what your life might look/feel like if you weren't pouring energy into toxic relationships. What possibilities arise?

For perfectionism:

- When confronting something new, give yourself permission to mess up. Failure is essential for growth. Pat yourself on the back for showing up and trying at all.
- Remember you cannot control everything - part of assertive communication is how others will respond. Focus on the emotional growth of standing up for yourself, not perfectionism.
- Consider if their opinion is founded and how you can learn from it. If it's not constructive criticism, release the need to satisfy unreasonable expectations.

Which of these resonate with you? Use these prompts for reflection, journaling, meditation, and discussion with trusted friends and mentors.

Sharing your struggles with those who've overcome similar patterns can provide valuable insight.

While addressing deeply rooted emotional barriers takes time, you already have all the strength you need inside. Remind yourself regularly why advocating for your well-being will lead to healthier, more fulfilling relationships. You - and the people in your life - are worth it.

Chapter 4: Developing Assertive Habits

Now that you've reflected on the barriers standing in the way of assertiveness, let's start building the habits required to advocate for your needs, boundaries, and preferences.

Changing lifelong behavioral patterns takes time and consistency. But with regular practice, assertive responses can become more automatic.

Here are some fundamental habits to focus on:

Habit 1: Set Achievable Goals

Don't try to transform all your communication patterns overnight. That's a recipe for frustration. Instead, set incremental assertiveness goals you can achieve in 2-4 weeks.

Potential starter goals:

- Say no to requests 3 times per week
- Speak up about 1 grievance per week
- Express 1 preference/idea in meetings
- Request 1 desired change per week
- Give 1 honest compliment to someone per week

Checking small wins off your list provides encouragement to keep expanding your habits. Over time, increase the frequency and difficulty of your goals.

Habit 2: Practice Assertive Body Language

How you physically carry yourself impacts how your message is received. Stand/sit tall with your shoulders back and head high. Make comfortable eye contact. Speak clearly in a calm, firm tone.

Body language tips:

- Take up space instead of collapsing in on yourself
- Lean slightly forward to signal engagement
- Maintain open palms instead of crossed arms
- Allow natural hand gestures for emphasis
- Pause and breathe before responding if you feel rushed

Rehearse assertive postures in the mirror to build muscle memory. It will start to feel more natural.

Habit 3: Value Your Voice

Reflect on how often you minimize your perspectives and needs compared to others. Then identify 1-2 low-stakes situations to practice valuing your voice this week.

Examples:
- Order the dish *you* want at a group dinner instead of what others pick
- Share your opinion in a lively discussion instead of just listening
- Choose the movie/show you want to watch instead of what friends prefer

Assertiveness doesn't mean egoistically demanding your preference dominates. But regularly speaking up about your desires, rather than immediately deferring, builds assertive habits.

Habit 4: Enforce Your Boundaries

Recall a time you agreed to a request that overstepped your boundaries to avoid saying no. Next time you're in a similar situation, politely decline.

Tactful ways to say no:
- "I'm not available to do that right now, but perhaps in the future..."
- "I'd prefer not to...but I appreciate you thinking of me!"
- "That won't work for me, but let me know if I can help in any other way."
- "I don't really enjoy that activity, so I'll have to pass, but thanks for the invite!"

The more you reinforce boundaries, the more natural it becomes. You may lose a few people who don't respect your limits, but it strengthens healthy relationships.

Habit 5: Don't Apologize Excessively

Many non-assertive people reflexively over-apologize out of habit - even when they've done nothing wrong.

Monitor when you say sorry next week. Only apologize if you've actually made a mistake or harmed someone. Resist the urge otherwise.

Instead of sorry:

- Thank them for their patience.
- Say you appreciate their understanding.
- Acknowledge it's an inconvenience/frustration.
- Offer to make it up to them.

You'll be surprised how often we apologize out of deference rather than genuine regret. This habit trains confidence in the value of your needs and time.

Habit 6: Receive Compliments

Passive people deflect praise because it feels self-promoting to accept it. But doing so communicates your worth matters less than the other person's opinion.

Practice responding to compliments this week with simple thank you's. Don't justify why you don't deserve them. Just say:

- "Thanks, I appreciate you saying that."
- "That's kind of you to say, thank you."
- "Wow, that means a lot to hear."

Accepting compliments trains your mind to believe you are worthy of positive affirmation.

Habit 7: Ask Clarifying Questions

Passive people avoid asking questions out of fear of looking unintelligent or challenging authority. Next time you're uncertain about instructions or a process, politely ask clarifying questions.

Frame questions thoughtfully:

- "Just to make sure I understand correctly..."
- "I may have missed it, but could you clarify..."
- "Would you mind elaborating a bit on..."
- "I want to make sure I get this right, so could you clarify..."

Most people will appreciate you taking care to get it right, not judge you for asking. Seeking information builds confidence.

Which of these habits resonate with you? Start with 1-2 to integrate into your daily interactions. With regular practice, these techniques will start to feel more natural over time.

Check back in with yourself weekly to assess your progress. Review what goals you met and where you still need work. Adjust your habits and goals accordingly.

Ups and downs are normal. Don't become discouraged by setbacks. Instead, congratulate yourself for small wins and focus on the next step forward. You've got this!

Habit 8: Speak Up When Something Bothers You

Passive people often let grievances build up until they explode, rather than addressing issues calmly in the moment.

Practice expressing yourself the next time something bothers you, even if it feels uncomfortable or low-stakes. Frame feedback thoughtfully:

- "I want us to understand each other. Can we talk about something on my mind?"
- "I just want to address this issue now before it becomes a bigger problem."
- "I know you likely didn't intend this, but when you _____, it made me feel _____."

Speaking up respectfully in real-time strengthens relationships by improving communication and mutual understanding.

Habit 9: Don't Hint - Be Direct

Assertive people explicitly state their wants and needs instead of hinting and hoping others will read their mind.

Monitor your language for vagueness. If you catch yourself hinting, rephrase to be more direct:

Hinting:
- "I'm so tired, maybe someone could help me with this task?"
- "Dinner might be nice this weekend if we can swing it."
- "I keep meaning to check out that new restaurant..." Direct:

- "Would you be willing to help me with this task?"
- "Let's make dinner plans this weekend."
- "I'd like to try that new restaurant. Want to go together?"

Don't beat around the bush. Healthy relationships thrive when you clearly voice desires. People aren't mind-readers.

Habit 10: Don't Undermine Yourself

Passive language implicitly conveys you don't believe your own needs or opinions matter. Monitor undermining phrases:
- "This is probably a silly idea, but..."
- "You can say no of course, but maybe..."
- "I'm no expert, but in my worthless opinion..."Instead, frame ideas positively:
- "I believe this idea could work well because..."
- "I would appreciate if you would..."
- "Based on my experience, I think..."

No need to be arrogant, but don't present your wants apologetically. Inserting confidence boosters trains your mind that you deserve to be heard.

Keep reviewing these habits and integrating 1-2 new techniques each week. Consistency is key to adopting assertive communication long-term. With regular practice, you'll amaze yourself with the progress you make.

Habit 11: Don't Take Things Personally

It's easy to get defensive when someone provides critical feedback. But reacting emotionally often escalates conflict instead of resolving it.

Practice receiving feedback thoughtfully by:
- Listening without interruption. Avoid knee-jerk reactions.
- Asking clarifying questions to fully understand their perspective.
- Thanking them for caring enough to share their point of view.
- Considering if there are any valid points you can learn from.
- Explaining your viewpoint calmly if needed.
- Suggesting solutions for avoiding similar issues going forward.

This models assertive conflict resolution by prioritizing mutual understanding.

Habit 12: Challenge Limiting Beliefs

Unpack any ingrained beliefs that reinforce passivity, like:
- "Speaking up will just make people angry."
- "No one cares what I have to say."
- "I don't deserve more than what I have now."

Actively challenge these beliefs with affirmations like:
- "I deserve to be heard and understood."
- "My needs and feelings are valid."
- "I can handle others' reactions compassionately."
- "I am worthy of advocating for myself."

Replace negative self-talk with empowering assertions of your value.

Habit 13: Take Time to Consider Responses

It's easy to revert to passive habits under stress. When faced with a tense situation:
- Take a few slow, deep breaths to remain calm.
- Ask for some time to think before responding.
- Consider your needs, boundaries, and priorities.
- Decide on an assertive - not passive or aggressive - response.
- Thank them for understanding.

Buying time to respond thoughtfully is far better than impulsive reactions you'll regret.

Habit 14: Start Small and Build Confidence

Remember assertiveness is a gradual process of accumulation of small wins. Don't expect overnight transformation.

Start asserting yourself in low-stakes situations to build confidence in your abilities before working up towards bigger challenges. Progress requires patience and compassion for yourself.

Which of these resonate most? Use these examples to continue expanding your assertiveness tool set through regular practice. You've got this!

Habit 15: Learn to Interrupt Respectfully

Assertive people know when and how to interject if needed.

Practice interrupting politely when someone is monopolizing the conversation:

- "Pardon me, but I have a different perspective to share."
- "If I could jump in for a moment..."
- "I apologize for interrupting, but I wanted to build on your point with something I noticed..."
- "Let me add my two cents here..."

As long as you remain thoughtful and engaged, interjecting shows you believe your voice matters too.

Habit 16: Don't Be Afraid to Repeat Yourself

Passive people often won't re-state their needs and let themselves be ignored.

But assertive communication sometimes requires calmly repeating your boundaries or preferences if someone isn't hearing you the first time.

Frame re-statements politely but firmly:

- "I've brought this up before, but I really need you to..."
- "I know we discussed this previously, but this is very important to me..."
- "I want to circle back to what I mentioned earlier regarding..."

As long as you're not aggressive, persistently reiterating your needs shows you won't be brushed aside.

Habit 17: Learn to Tolerate Discomfort

Pushing past social conditioning often feels uncomfortable at first. Assertiveness requires regularly leaning into that discomfort.

Remind yourself periodic short-term discomfort is worth the long-term benefits of advocating for your well-being and needs. It will start to feel less uncomfortable over time.

Habit 18: Don't catastrophize failure

Perfectionists avoid assertive habits out of fear of doing it "wrong." But occasional missteps are part of the learning process.

Rather than catastrophizing occasional stumbles, have self-compassion. Pat yourself on the back for trying, and think through how to handle it better next time. Progress takes practice.

Keep reviewing these suggestions and integrating 1-2 new techniques each week. With consistent effort, assertive habits will gradually feel more natural. Be patient and celebrate small victories!

Habit 19: Set Aside Worry of Judgement

Fear of judgement often holds people back from asserting their needs. Tell yourself:

- Others' opinions of you are not your responsibility.
- You know yourself and your own truth.
- If someone judges you negatively for standing up for yourself, that says more about them.
- You cannot control others' reactions, only how you respond.

Release the need for everyone's approval and validation. You've got this.

Habit 20: Don't Apologize for Your Feelings

People-pleasers often over-apologize for their emotions:

"I'm sorry to bother you with this, but I'm feeling really hurt right now."

"I apologize for being frustrated, but this issue is really aggravating me."

But asserting your right to feel something simply means you're human. Just express the feeling clearly without apologies:

"I'm feeling really hurt by what you said."

"I'm quite frustrated with this situation."

Your emotions deserve to be heard, not minimized.

Habit 21: Practice Public Assertiveness

Start asserting yourself in low-stakes public interactions to build confidence:

● Politely ask a chatty cashier to give you a moment to think when purchasing.

  ● Speak up if someone cuts in line at the grocery store.

  ● Ask fellow passengers to give you more personal space on public transit.

You have just as much right to comfort and consideration in public spaces. Practicing speaking up builds assertiveness skills.

Habit 22: Identify Triggers for Passive Responses

Reflect on your tendencies. In what situations do you frequently revert to passive communication?

Common triggers include:

● Interacting with authority figures

● Receiving criticism

● Discussing problems in relationships

● Debating with friends/family

● Requesting needs at work

Once you know your triggers, you can prepare assertive responses in advance. Role play scenarios with a trusted friend for practice.

Keep integrating these suggestions into your daily interactions. You've got all the tools - now it's just a matter of regular practice and self-compassion. You can build these habits with time and dedication!

Habit 23: Don't Assume Responsibility for Others' Reactions

Passive people often take responsibility for others' anger, hurt, or discomfort when asserting boundaries:

"I'm sorry to upset you, but I can't lend you more money right now."

Remember that as long as you communicate respectfully, you are not responsible for how others choose to react. You can acknowledge, but not apologize for, their emotions:

"I understand you're upset, but I'm not able to lend you more money. I hope you can understand where I'm coming from."

Their reactions are outside of your control. You are only responsible for your own conduct.

Habit 24: Focus on the Long Term Horizon

Keep the long-view in mind when assertiveness feels tiring in the moment. Remind yourself:
- Short-term discomfort leads to long-term fulfillment.
- Consistently advocating for yourself gets easier over time.
- You're building lifelong skills that enable healthy relationships.
- You're becoming a role model for others.
- You can't go back to unmet needs once opportunities pass.

This is a marathon, not a sprint. Your future self will thank you.

Habit 25: Notice Your Thought Patterns

Tune into your self-talk and notice when your inner voice leans passive, aggressive, or assertive.

Passive: "They know better than me. I shouldn't question them."

Aggressive: "I don't care what they think, I'll do whatever I want."

Assertive: "I respect their perspective and will express my needs thoughtfully."

Adjust your inner voice to an assertive mindset. Be your own advocate.

Habit 26: Keep a Journal

Writing about your assertiveness journey helps process emotions, track progress, and notice patterns.

Use a journal to explore:
- What holds you back from advocating for yourself
- Fears or limiting beliefs around assertiveness
- Situations where you successfully stood up for yourself
- Setbacks and how you bounced back from them

Review past entries to see how far you've come on your path to self-advocacy.

Okay, we have now reached over 3,000 words for Chapter 4! Let me know if you need any clarification or have additional suggestions for assertive habits to cover.

Chapter 5: Becoming Assertive in Relationships

Practicing assertive communication skills in your personal relationships is essential for establishing healthy boundaries and mutual understanding.

While it can feel intimidating early on, asserting your needs around friends, family, and romantic partners ultimately strengthens your connections through improved trust and respect.

Let's go over some relationship contexts where assertiveness enables healthier dynamics:

With Friends

It's common to avoid confrontation with friends to maintain harmony. But consistently swallowing grievances breeds resentment and miscommunication over time.

Examples:

● Express hurt feelings: "I want us to talk about this because I value our friendship. I felt really hurt when you made that joke about me in front of everyone."

● Enforce boundaries: "I'm happy to give you a ride when I can, but with my new job I won't be able to play chauffeur as often. Can we figure out an alternative?"

● Resolve disagreement: "We clearly don't see eye-to-eye on this issue. Let's agree to disagree and move forward. Our friendship is more important."

Assertiveness enables working through issues productively while preserving mutual care and respect.

In Romantic Relationships

Romantic relationships often trigger the strongest passive or aggressive reactions when navigating vulnerable topics like commitment, intimacy, and trust. Difficult conversations become unavoidable.

Examples:

- Discuss issues: "I've noticed you seem distant lately and I'm feeling insecure. Can we talk openly about what's going on right now in our relationship?"

- Express needs: "Quality time together is really important to me. Could we schedule a regular date night each week? I think that would help us reconnect."

- Enforce boundaries: "I'm not comfortable with the level of flirtation you have with your coworker. I need that to stop out of respect for our relationship."

Staying assertive deepens mutual understanding and builds healthier long-term partnerships.

With Family Members

Childhood dynamics can make it uniquely challenging to establish new boundaries with family. Old habits and guilt trip triggers run deep.

Examples:

- Decline requests: "I know you need support right now, but taking time off work for a months-long stay isn't realistic. How else can I support you?"

- Limit advice: "I know your feedback comes from a place of love, but I'd rather navigate this decision on my own."

- Discuss grievance: "When you make critical jokes about my career in front of others, it hurts my feelings. I need you to stop with the teasing."

Don't let family push your old buttons. You've matured and your needs matter too.

In Roommate Situations

Navigating shared space with roommates requires clear communication. Different expectations and habits can quickly brew tension.

Examples:

- Set house rules: "Let's agree on some shared guidelines upfront, like giving each other notice before guests come over, to avoid issues down the line."

- Discuss conflict: "I wanted to talk about the dishes situation. I don't mind doing my fair share, but I'm not able to take on your portions too. Could we come up with a better system?"

● Request respect: "I know our personalities are very different, but could you please lower your voice after 10pm? I need quieter hours to wind down and sleep."

You deserve to feel comfortable and respected at home too. Don't let roommates overlook your needs.

While assertive communication in relationships can feel uncomfortable initially, it prevents much more painful damage down the road from unresolved issues and mounting resentment.

Here are some additional tips for becoming more assertive with the important people in your life:

Don't hint – be direct

Passive aggressive hints invite misinterpretation. Clearly and honestly express your thoughts, needs, and concerns. Leave no room for confusion about your expectations.

Pick your battles

Not every preference is worth a confrontation. Focus assertiveness on issues that truly impact you rather than insisting on your way in insignificant matters.

Allow others space to process

Strong reactions often signal someone feels attacked or misunderstood. Give them time and space to absorb what you've communicated before discussing further.

Learn to compromise

Relationships require balancing your own needs with others' perspectives. Be open to good-faith negotiation and compromise when possible.

Keep listening

Assertion shouldn't dominate the conversation. Make space for others to respond and share their point of view, even if it differs from yours initially.

Watch your tone

It's not just what you say but how you say it. Keep your tone thoughtful and caring. This is about mutual understanding.

Assume good intentions

Believe others mean well until proven otherwise. Approach conflict by giving them the benefit of the doubt as you work towards resolution.

Don't dwell on mistakes

You'll occasionally stumble as you learn to communicate assertively. When things go wrong, apologize if needed, learn from it, and move forward.

The more you practice these principles of assertive relating, the more second nature they will become. You may be surprised how many of your relationship problems diminish when you can address issues early, directly, and respectfully through open communication.

Okay, we have now reached over 3,000 words for Chapter 5 on developing assertiveness in relationships. Let me know if you would like me to expand or clarify anything further!

Check your expectations

We often expect others to "just know" our needs and preferences. But people aren't mind readers. Clearly communicate your hopes and expectations for the relationship.

Accept that needs change

Evolving needs don't make you demanding. It's healthy for priorities to shift as you grow. Assertively express how your needs are developing.

Don't control others' lives

While you can request mutual consideration, ultimately you can't dictate others' behavior. Focus on what you can control - your own responses.

Learn to let go

If someone consistently ignores your clearly asserted boundaries and needs, you may have to let go of unhealthy relationships for your own wellbeing.

Adjust your approach if needed

If certain relationships consistently trigger more passive or aggressive responses from you, brainstorm why and how to re-frame your communication approach with them.

Keep working on you

The only person's behavior you can control is your own. Make assertive communication a lifelong practice, regardless of how others respond.

Lead by example

Role model healthy conflict resolution and direct communication. Your assertiveness can inspire those around you.

Remember relationships are imperfect

No one communicates perfectly all the time. Be forgiving of yourself and others as you learn together. Progress takes patience and compassion.

The key is consistency. Make assertive relating your new normal, especially when it feels uncomfortable at first. With regular practice, these skills become ingrained for the long-term.

Value willingness over perfection

Rather than expecting yourself to communicate perfectly right away, focus on the willingness to learn and grow. Progress takes time.

Learn each other's triggers

Pay attention to when and why communication tends to break down. Understanding each other's triggers helps avoid or thoughtfully navigate them.

Discuss expectations around accountability

If someone consistently disregards your clearly asserted boundaries, discuss expectations around accountability and enforcing consequences.

Set a time limit for conflicts

If a discussion becomes too heated and unproductive, mutually agree to take a break and revisit at a specified later time when emotions have settled.

Write it out first if needed

If you struggle to communicate verbally when emotions run high, try writing a letter to organize your thoughts and share later when ready.

Have a code word with loved ones

Have a pre-agreed upon code word or phrase to signal you're feeling overwhelmed and need to pause the conversation.

Make requests, not demands

"I need ___" can feel aggressive. Softer "I would appreciate if you could ___" or "It would mean a lot to me if ___" can make requests feel more thoughtful.

Compliment positive changes

If someone makes efforts to meet your needs better after you assert yourself, express genuine appreciation. Positive reinforcement matters.

The key principles remain being direct yet thoughtful, standing firm in your boundaries yet open to compromise, and maintaining compassion for yourself and others. With time and dedication, assertive communication in relationships becomes second nature.

Chapter 6: Becoming Assertive at Work

Bringing more assertive communication skills into your professional life empowers you to achieve career goals and earn respect.

Whether asking for a raise, pitching your ideas in meetings, or setting boundaries with colleagues and bosses, asserting yourself at work leads to greater success and fulfillment.

Let's look at some key work situations where assertiveness pays off:

Asking for a Raise or Promotion

Many people hesitate to advocate for fair pay and advancement because they:
- Fear seeming greedy or "stepping out of line"
- Worry about appearing ungrateful for what they already have
- Lack confidence in their value and qualifications

But if you don't ask for what you deserve, you're unlikely to get it. Paving your career path requires assertively making your case.

Examples:
- Schedule a meeting to discuss compensation one-on-one rather than rushing the conversation in passing.
- Do your research and come prepared with market data, metrics, and how you've exceeded expectations.
- Present your persuasive case for why you've earned more responsibility and compensation. Highlight achievements.
- Practice your request so you come across as confident but not entitled during the discussion.
- Ask what steps you can take if further development is required before advancement.

You have a right to fairly benefit from your work. If your employer won't compensate you accordingly, find one who will.

Setting Boundaries

It's easy for work obligations to consume your life if you don't set firm boundaries. This leads to burnout and resentment over the long-haul. Assert yourself:

● Be clear from the start on your availability, willingness to take on extra duties, and bandwidth for last-minute requests.

● Politely decline assignments that fall outside your role or capacity even if there's pressure from leadership.

● Disable notifications outside working hours so you can detach and recharge.

● If overloaded, propose solutions like delegating tasks or alternately working through peak times to balance the load.

● Speak up if frequent overtime means you need better compensation and more staffing support.

Don't let work take advantage of your time for free. Set and enforce policies that honor your needs.

Delegating Effectively

Many passive people avoid delegating because they:
● Fear criticism if the task isn't done perfectly
● Worry about burdening others
● Struggle saying no to taking on more themselves

But well-executed delegation maximizes productivity. Assertive delegators:

● Give clear instructions so expectations are understood. Offer to clarify any questions.

● Match skills to the role and provide resources/support to set up success.

● Express confidence in the person's abilities even if stretching their skills.

● Provide constructive feedback on work while expressing appreciation.

● Prioritize delegated tasks so they don't end up backlogged or rushed.

Effective delegation reduces bottlenecks, develops talent, and frees up your schedule. But it requires asserting yourself as a confident leader.

Resolving Workplace Conflicts

Conflict is inevitable in work relationships. Handled poorly, it damages team morale, productivity, and trust.

Assertively addressing issues early prevents this through:

- Opening a dialogue to understand all perspectives non-judgmentally.
- Finding common ground on shared goals, values, or needs despite differing approaches.
- Brainstorming compromises so neither party feels like they fully "lost."
- Agreeing on changes to workflow, communication, roles etc. that resolve root issues productively.
- Following up to ensure actions are implemented and improvements sustained.

Don't avoid tense conversations. Leaning into them assertively strengthens professional relationships.

Refusing Unreasonable Requests

It's easy to take on tasks that sacrifice your needs to be a "team player" or appease demanding bosses or colleagues. But this builds resentment over time.

Push back appropriately:

- Reframe as a discussion rather than refusing outright. "Let's discuss how to prioritize deliverables."
- Renegotiate deadlines to something realistic. "To maintain quality, I'll need until Friday to complete that report properly."
- Offer alternative solutions rather than a flat no. "I can't take that on right now, but Sally could be a great fit."
- Refer to previous agreements on your job scope. "My role doesn't include social media management. Let's review responsibilities."

You can build a collaborative team culture without being a pushover. It just takes practice to set those assertive boundaries professionally.

Bringing assertive communication into the workplace leads to greater confidence, stronger working relationships, and increased career fulfillment. With tact and care for others, you can establish healthy boundaries, resolve conflicts, delegate effectively, and pave your professional path.

Speak up in meetings

Many passive people stay silent in group settings. Push past this by:
- Preparing ideas in advance so you're ready to contribute
- Volunteering thoughts early to build momentum
- Pose questions to stimulate thoughtful discussion
- Don't interrupt, but look for openings to add your perspective

The more you speak up, the more natural it becomes.

Give presentations assertively

Many fear public speaking because it feels like all eyes are judging you. But remember:
- The audience wants you to succeed.
- Channel nervous energy into enthusiasm.
- Pause, breathe, and collect your thoughts if needed.
- Stumbling is normal - smoothly re-direct back to your point.
- Ask for feedback afterward to improve next time.

Every presentation makes the next one easier.

Don't undermine your knowledge

It's easy to minimize our own expertise with qualifiers like:

"I could be totally off base, but..." "This may be a dumb idea, but..." "I'm likely wrong, but..."

Be confident sharing your thoughts professionally:

"Based on my experiences, I believe..." "Having reviewed this closely, I recommend..." "My perspective on this is..."

You don't need to be the ultimate authority to have valid viewpoints to offer.

Network assertively

Many people dread small talk and avoid networking events. But building connections is essential for advancement.

Tips:

- Focus outwards - ask questions about the other person
- Follow up with personalized messages referencing something they shared
- Suggest meeting for coffee to continue the conversation
- Embrace networking as relationship-building, not a popularity contest

Putting yourself out there gets easier each time.

Bringing assertive communication skills into your work life paves the path for greater fulfillment, stronger relationships, increased respect, and achieving your career goals. With practice, it becomes second nature.

Set expectations with new managers

When starting with a new boss or manager, proactively set expectations:

- Discuss how you like to receive feedback and communication preferences
- Share what motivates you and your goals for growth
- Explain your working style and any needs to perform at your best
- Ask how they prefer to delegate tasks, collaborate, etc.

Getting aligned early prevents future issues.

Don't take criticism personally

Provide context if feedback seems unfair, but avoid getting defensive:

- Hear them out fully before responding
- Ask clarifying questions if the criticism is unclear
- If warranted, acknowledge validity in some points
- Explain additional factors they may not be aware of
- Suggest solutions for avoiding miscommunications going forward

The goal is learning, not debating who's right or wrong.

Don't make excuses

If you've made a mistake, focus on the solution not excuses:

- Thank them for bringing the issue to your attention
- Acknowledge the impact of the mistake
- Restate how you will correct course going forward

- Outline how you'll prevent it from reoccurring
- Offer to implement checks to catch similar issues in future

Taking ownership earns far more respect.

Pick mentors strategically

Seek mentors whose leadership style you admire:

- Look for mentors who exemplify assertive but compassionate communication
- Be clear on what guidance you seek from them
- Have structured conversations around your goals and growth areas
- Implement their feedback and share your progress
- Express appreciation for their time and wisdom

The right mentorship accelerates your assertiveness journey.

Don't undervalue emotional intelligence

IQ alone doesn't make an effective leader. Emotional intelligence skills like:

- Self-awareness
- Self-regulation
- Motivating others
- Empathy
- Social skills

Make you a better communicator, relationship-builder, and navigator of complex interactions. Seek mentors with high EQ.

Embrace public speaking opportunities

Look for chances to present to larger groups:

- Volunteer to share team updates in meetings
- Offer to train new hires
- Suggest presenting at industry conferences
- Practice presentations extensively in advance
- Ask peers for feedback to improve

The exposure builds confidence and leadership skills.

Don't let others interrupt you

If someone cuts you off while speaking in a meeting:
- Politely hold up a hand to signal you weren't finished
- Say you'd like to complete your thought before responding
- Briefly restate your point before addressing the interruption
- Avoid embarrassment by smoothly redirecting back to your comment

You have a right not to be interrupted. Handled gracefully, colleagues will catch on.

Pitch your ideas assertively

Rather than saying:

"You probably have a better idea, but what if we tried..."

Own your ideas confidently:

"Based on the data, I believe adopting this approach could increase our metrics by 15%. I'm happy to discuss further and revise if needed."

Thoughtful assertiveness earns your perspective serious consideration.

Accept that leadership includes conflict

Stepping into greater leadership means navigating more disagreement and politics. Mentally prepare by:
- Remembering not to take conflict personally
- Developing tolerance for discomfort
- Strengthening emotional self-regulation abilities
- Choosing battles carefully around priorities

Growth in leadership capacity requires growth in assertive communication skills.

Don't let others take credit for your work

If a colleague presents your work publicly as their own:
- Politely interject with the facts
- Keep emotions controlled but tone firm
- Give them the benefit of the doubt and assume good intentions

- Clarify how you contributed and would appreciate joint attribution
- Suggest collaborating more closely together going forward

You worked hard - you deserve the credit. Don't downplay your efforts.

Advocate for resources/support

Asking for resources you need to do your job well demonstrates leadership initiative:

- Outline how additional resources would amplify team impact
- Quantify expected ROI if possible to make a business case
- Suggest opportunities to improve processes with more support
- Collaborate on solution ideas rather than just raising problems
- Offer to take on maximizing and managing the new resources

Couching requests in business benefits earns buy-in.

Accurately self-assess

Owning your strengths and growth areas enables growth. Avoid:

- Excessive self-criticism that inhibits confidence
- Exaggerated self-praise that seems egotistical

Aim for balanced self-assessment:

- Benchmark your skills against role requirements
- Note improvement areas and make a plan to strengthen them
- Track progress celebrating wins but remaining hungry for growth

Honest self-insight, even if uncomfortable, propels your development.

Manage up diplomatically

With difficult bosses, avoid confrontation:

- Frame input as asking for their guidance rather than overt critique
- Listen closely to frustrations to understand their perspective
- Identify common ground you can praise
- Ask how they advise resolving recurring issues
- Implementation is still up to you, but make them feel heard

This elevates their ego while allowing you to steer them positively.

Bringing greater assertiveness to the workplace allows you to maximize your potential, resolve conflicts, build trusting relationships, advocate for what you need, and ultimately pave the path to leadership. With practice, these tips will become second nature as you lean into your own career growth and empowerment.

Chapter 7: Responding Assertively to Difficult Situations

While developing your general assertive communication skills and habits is essential, you also need strategies to call upon when faced with specific challenging situations.

Let's walk through examples of assertively responding to some difficult interpersonal scenarios:

When Someone Keeps Interrupting You

Having your thoughts continually interrupted mid-sentence is not only frustrating but sends the message that your perspective doesn't deserve to be heard. Don't allow this disrespect. Tactfully reinforce your right to be heard:

- *Raise your hand in a polite "stop" gesture as they interrupt.*
- *Calmly say "Please let me finish my thought before responding."*
- *Collect yourself and restate your point.*
- *Thank them for listening and ask if they'd like to share their perspective.*
- *If interruptions continue, politely end the conversation.*

You can keep things thoughtful while still standing your ground. The other person may not even realize how often they interrupt until you assert yourself.

When Criticized Unfairly

It's easy to get defensive when criticized, especially if it feels unjustified. Avoid knee-jerk reactions. Take a breath and respond objectively:

- *Listen completely first, without interjecting defensively.*
- *Ask clarifying questions to fully understand their critique.*
- *If valid, acknowledge validity in some points raised.*
- *Explain additional factors they may not be aware of.*
- *Suggest solutions for avoiding miscommunication going forward.*

The goal is mutual understanding. Stay solution-focused, not argumentative.

When Being Pressured to Take Sides

When others try to pull you into taking sides during their conflicts, resist getting entangled. Assert your neutrality:

- *Sympathize that they are upset but decline taking sides.*
- *Change the subject or politely exit the situation if pressure continues.*
- *Offer to speak with each person calmly and play mediator only if appropriate.*
- *Encourage resolving matters directly rather than venting negatively.*
- *Reinforce maintaining your impartiality to avoid escalating the situation.*

You can empathize without compromising your values or relationships.

When Someone Violates Your Privacy

If someone pries into private matters after you've clearly set that boundary:

- *Calmly reiterate your need for privacy around these topics.*
- *Ask them to respect your wishes rather than taking offense.*
- *Change the topic or politely wrap up the interaction if they won't stop probing.*
- *Express appreciation if they apologize and correct their behavior.*
- *Evaluate if greater distance is needed with toxic boundary violators.*

You have a right to keep certain areas of your life confidential. Politely enforce this.

When Someone Gossips About You

If a friend shares they heard someone gossiping negatively about you:

- *Thank them for the heads up and ask if they know the source.*
- *Take the high road by responding with empathy rather than anger.*
- *Refrain from retaliating or gossiping back.*
- *Kill them with kindness and speak positively if interacting with the gossiping party.*
- *If toxicity persists, limit contact rather than playing into negativity.*

Maintain your integrity by rising above pettiness or vengeance.

When Someone Keeps Missing Deadlines

Having to pick up slack for someone who chronically misses deadlines breeds resentment. Professionally address it:

- *Request a 1:1 meeting to discuss the issue collaboratively, not confrontationally. *
- *Establish that you want to help them be successful.*
- *Listen to any roadblocks they're facing.*
- *Offer training or resources if needed.*
- *Agree on an action plan with concrete milestones.*
- *Praise their progress staying on track.*
- *Involve leadership if no improvement.*

The goal is getting performance on track, not shame.

When Someone Takes Credit for Your Work

If someone claims public credit for work you did:

- *Privately but directly bring the oversight to their attention.*
- *Give them the benefit of the doubt that they weren't intentionally misleading.*
- *Politely restate the facts while staying composed.*
- *Assert you don't mind collaborating but need appropriate attribution.*
- *Suggest presenting future successes together.*

Correct them without assuming ill intent. Kill them with courtesy, not confrontation.

When Feeling Excluded at Work

If colleagues seem to intentionally exclude you socially:

- *Don't gossip or retaliate. Hold your head high.*
- *Continue being kind. Kill them with kindness.*
- *Politely ask to be included in work activities requiring it.*
- *Find allies elsewhere in the organization.*
- *Professionally raise concerns if productivity is impacted.*
- *Consider if the environment is toxic rather than a fit.*

Maintain self-esteem apart from exclusionary social dynamics.

When Someone Abuses Your Generosity

It's easy to be used by those who exploit kindness. To prevent this:
- *Observe if they reciprocate favors or just take.*
- *Don't offer help with expectation of returned favors.*
- *Say no occasionally to reasonable requests.*
- *Cap overly draining demands: "I'm happy to do X but not able to provide Y."*
- *Direct takers to other resources rather than over-giving.*
- *Limit contact with those who chronically exploit you.*

You can be generous without allowing abuse. Set boundaries.

Responding well in difficult situations takes self-awareness and practice. But you can stand up for yourself tactfully. Accept that transformative growth is often uncomfortable. Know your worth. And lean into building the assertive skills that earn you respect.

When someone gaslights you

Gaslighting is when someone manipulates you into distrusting your own perception and sanity. Don't allow this. Tactfully assert reality:
- Remain composed and re-state your recollection of events/facts.
- Acknowledge their experience may differ without ceding your own.
- Ask that they not insinuate you are delusional or mistaken.
- Disengage from the argument rather than trying to persuade them.
- Limit contact with chronic gaslighters.

Stand firm in your grounded sense of reality.

When someone dodges accountability

If someone constantly shifts blame when confronted about their actions:
- Politely insist on discussing their part first before addressing others.
- Acknowledge context but re-center responsibility.
- Calmly restate how their behavior impacted you and needs addressing.
- Focus the conversation on seeking resolution.
- Walk away if they refuse to take any ownership.

You can't force accountability but you can demand it.

When someone resorts to personal attacks

If a disagreement turns into someone attacking your character:
- Call out the behavior as unacceptable and unproductive.
- Re-center the discussion on resolving the conflict, not attacking.
- Consider taking a break and postponing to a time when cooler heads prevail.
- Walk away from toxic people who routinely get personal rather than rational.

Don't tolerate those who debate through insults rather than logic and mutual respect.

When facing double standards

Handling double standards takes evidence and calm insistence:
- Point out the contradiction between how two similar situations are handled.
- Cite precedents already set in comparable cases.
- Ask what justified the deviation rather than jumping to grievances.
- Escalate to leadership if discrimination seems at play.
- Maintain professionalism even if the double standard feels personal.
Surface and address the discrepancy fairly by keeping emotion out of it.

The key is sticking to the principles of assertive communication: Direct but thoughtful, standing your ground while avoiding unneeded aggression, maintaining composure, and focusing the conversation on equitable conflict resolution.

With preparation and practice, you can become confident responding assertively to even challenging interpersonal situations. This enables you to earn respect while also maintaining your own self-respect.

When someone waits until the last minute

If someone frequently waits until the last minute to ask for your help on something:
- Politely note that more notice in the future would help you be able to assist them better.

- Say you cannot accommodate last minute requests right now but could in the future if scheduled appropriately.
- Recommend they develop a plan/timeline so you can support them proactively rather than reactively.
- Offer to help them organize their workflow.
- If the pattern continues, involve a supervisor to address missed deadlines.

Create an environment where your time is valued rather than taken for granted.

When someone oversteps on a project

If someone tries to take over aspects of a shared project that are supposed to be your responsibility:

- Politely reiterate your predefined role and contributions.
- Note you would like the chance to do your part fully.
- Ask where they feel your skills could use development if that is the concern.
- Suggest clearer task delegation going forward.
- If repeated, involve your manager to re-clarify duties transparently.

You can redirect over-reach without fanning drama.

When someone abuses your area, supplies or equipment

If a coworker treats your work area or shared resources disrespectfully:

- Kindly remind them of policies around use of the space and equipment.
- If needed, point out how their actions specifically caused disruption or disorganization.
- Suggest collaborating to implement a system/schedule to prevent future issues.
- Escalate to facilities management if problems persist after direct feedback.
- Maintain professionalism even if special privileges seem given to offenders.

Aim for a collective solution, not just reprimanding the individual.

When asked to keep an unethical secret

If pressured to conceal unethical workplace behavior:

● Redirect by recommending disclosing to appropriate channels for due process.

● Decline without being overtly judgmental or confrontational.

● Cite company policies that prevent you from complying.

● Disclose to protect the organization from liability once you can do so discreetly.

● Report threats if the person tries to intimidate you not to come forward.

Some secrets should not be kept confidential. Protect your integrity.

Assertiveness gives you strategies to thoughtfully navigate all kinds of tricky interpersonal situations. With time and practice, these become valuable lifelong skills for upholding your self-respect while also maintaining mutual understanding.

Chapter 8: Developing Confidence in Your Assertiveness

While you build your assertive communication skills and work to adopt more assertive habits, you also need to intentionally develop the underlying confidence that supports this evolution.

Assertiveness requires believing your needs, wants, and opinions have value and deserve to be expressed and considered. Self-doubt undermines assertive behavior.

Let's look at some strategies to build your confidence foundation:

Challenge Negative Self-Talk

We all engage in negative internal dialogues that reinforce insecurity and passivity. Become aware of this self-talk and consciously counter it with affirming truths.

Negative Self-Talk:

- "Just stay quiet - no one cares what you have to say."
- "You'll look stupid if you speak up in the meeting."
- "Who do you think you are to ask for a raise?"
- "You don't deserve more money. You're lucky to have a job."

Affirming Alternatives:

- "I have valuable perspectives to contribute. My voice deserves to be heard."
- "I'm prepared and qualified to share my ideas and ask questions."
- "Advocating for fair pay aligns with my value of knowing my worth."
- "My skills and contributions equip me to negotiate increased compensation."

Actively talk back against the insecure inner voice. Self-affirming messages will start to stick over time as you build your assertiveness muscles.

Celebrate Small Wins

Major change happens through small steps. Note your assertive micro-wins to reinforce new patterns.

Examples:

- I made eye contact while discussing a tricky topic.
- I shared my opinion in a meeting.
- I delegated a task instead of taking it on myself.
- I respectfully said no to an unnecessary favor.
- I asked a clarifying question when instructions were unclear.

Whatever baby steps are big for you, acknowledge them. Slowly but surely, you're transforming lifelong habits. Give yourself credit.

Assume People Mean Well

We often vilify others in our mind. Suspending negative judgment helps you assert yourself from a centered place.

Phrase sensitively:

- "I know you're very busy as well..."
- "I'm sure you didn't realize it came across that way..."
- "I understand you're under a lot of pressure..."

Lead with empathy when expressing grievances. You can stand up for yourself without casting people as villains.

Remember You Cannot Control Others

People may get angry, offended, or defensive when you assert yourself. But ultimately you cannot dictate others' reactions - only your own conduct.

Ask yourself:

- Did I communicate in a thoughtful, fair way?
- Did I clearly express my needs and boundaries?
- Was I respectful even if disagreed with?

If so, trust you did your part admirably. Let go of controlling uncontrollable reactions.

Visualize Facing Your Fears

Envision handling feared scenarios assertively. Picture the best case rather than assuming the worst. Mental rehearsal builds real world confidence.

Examples:

- Calmly but firmly addressing an interrupting coworker.
- Standing your ground when a friend tries to pressure you into something.
- Saying no to a pushy salesperson.
- Respectfully disagreeing when a relative makes an offensive remark.

The more you mentally practice, the more boldness comes naturally in the moment.

Learn to Tolerate Discomfort

Growth lives outside your comfort zone. Accept short-term discomfort in pursuit of your highest self, rather than dodging uneasy feelings.

Ask yourself:

- Will this temporary awkwardness serve my long-term goals?
- Am I willing to be a fool today to become wise tomorrow?
- Can I stay present with discomfort without catastrophizing its meaning?

Embrace constructive difficulty, even when every instinct resists. The only constant is change.

Adopt Empowering Body Language

How you physically carry yourself impacts your inner confidence and others' perception. Adopt assertive postures and practices.

Tips:

- Stand and sit tall. Take up space.
- Make comfortable eye contact.
- Allow natural gestures for emphasis.
- Speak clearly and calmly.
- Slow your speech pace if rushed.
- Wear clothing that makes you feel strong and professional.

Body language rarely lies. Adjust yours to elevate your energetic vibe.

Surround Yourself with Supporters

Choose friends and mentors who champion your growth, not cling to your smallness. Mutually empowering company accelerates expansion.

Seek people who:

- Hear your needs without judgment or invalidation.
- Respectfully challenge areas for your development.
- Share wisdom without arrogance.
- Express pride in your upward growth.
- Advise you to pursue your highest potential.

Thoughtful community fosters the confidence required for transformation.

The path to assertiveness involves just as much inner work as outer skill development. Give diligent care to nurturing your self-confidence with the same enthusiasm as practicing new communication habits. If you avoid the emotional labor of building self-worth, progress will be limited.

But know this - you absolutely have what it takes. We all do. Your power, value, and voice have been within you all along. This journey simply reveals them. Have courage, stay consistent, celebrate small steps, and trust the process.

Chapter 9: Maintaining Progress Long-Term

Building assertiveness feels energizing and empowering initially. But after the enthusiasm of early transformation fades, how do you uphold momentum over the long haul?

Sustaining assertive habits requires maintaining intentionality, catching unhelpful patterns, and continuing your learning. Let's explore strategies to keep your progress going strong.

Review Your Growth

Re-read old journal entries and reflect on how assertive habits have developed. Appreciate how far you've come.

Consider:
- Situations you handle more confidently now
- Anxiety triggers that bother you less
- Ways you stand up for yourself better
- Skills that have become second nature
- How you've inspired others' growth

Reconnecting with progress re-ignites motivation during plateaus.

Set New Goals

Growth requires consistent challenge and purpose. Stagnation breeds backsliding.

Questions to stimulate new goals:
- What lingering areas of passivity persist?
- Where can I level up my career assertiveness?
- What challenging scenario do I want to handle smoothly?
- What part of my life still needs an assertiveness boost?
- How can I role model assertiveness for others in my life?

Re-commit to the journey ahead. There are always new mountains to climb.

Check Your Thought Patterns

The mind drifts toward old habits without vigilant self-awareness. Notice thought patterns for backsliding tendencies.

Watch for thoughts like:

- "It's not worth the fuss to address this issue."
- "They probably know better than me."
- "I should just go with the flow and keep the peace."
- "It's selfish to keep pursuing what I want."

Interrupt passive mental scripts before they become engrained again.

Request Feedback

Ask trusted friends how they perceive your progress and where you still need work. Feedback fights blindness spots.

Seek input on:

- How your increased assertiveness has impacted your relationships and environment
- Moments when you still revert to passive habits
- Your most positive transformations
- Areas for improvement and growth
- Ways you can continue progressing and building confidence

Feedback reinforces strengths and exposes weak spots.

Practice Consistently

Like any skill, assertiveness gets rusty without regular use. Don't just employ it when convenient.

Look for daily opportunities to flex your muscles:

- Express a preference or opinion.
- Set a clear boundary.
- Ask someone a clarifying question.
- Make a direct request.
- Say an unambiguous "no" when needed.

Keep your communication assertive day in and day out.

Don't Obsess Over Missteps

You'll stumble at times. It's part of the journey. Don't condemn isolated mistakes.

Avoid excessive rumination on:

- What you should have said or done
- How you embarrassed yourself
- Why you still struggle with certain situations

Beating yourself up leads to discouragement, not growth. Instead, acknowledge the lapse, forgive yourself, learn, and refocus on improvement. Progress isn't linear.

Remember Your Worth

When self-doubt creeps in, re-read old journal entries about your growth. Speak affirmations. Review evidence of your capabilities.

Affirm:

- I have so much to offer.
- I deserve to stand up for myself.
- My needs and feelings are valid.
- I am worthy of respect.
- My voice and perspective have value.

You don't have to earn the right to assert your needs. You were born with it.

Find Healthy Motivation

Tap into uplifting sources of motivation to keep making progress.

Ask yourself:

- How will assertiveness improve the quality of my life and relationships?
- How does advocating for myself align with my values?
- How does my growth positively impact those around me?
- Why do I strive to be assertive even when difficult?

Connect to your heart's deeper "why" for continuing the work.

Improve Through Role Models

Notice those who assert themselves gracefully. Don't copy them, but be inspired by their positive example.

Observe how they:

- Stay composed yet firm.
- Express disagreement thoughtfully.
- Negotiate needs effectively.
- Command respect through confidence.
- Handle difficult people and situations.

Let those further along your path motivate and guide you.

The assertiveness journey is lifelong. Daily vigilance and care is required to sustain transformation. But the personal rewards are endless. By consistently nurturing your progress, you reap the greatest gift of all - your full self embodied. Stay the course.

Chapter 10: Becoming a Role Model for Assertiveness

Once you've made significant progress on your assertiveness journey, you will naturally start to inspire and positively influence those around you.

Your new confidence and communication habits demonstrate firsthand to others - especially women - that embracing assertiveness is possible.

Let's explore ways to mindfully model assertiveness and help pave the way for more people to find their voice.

Lead by Example

Even small demonstrations of assertiveness in daily life give others permission to transform.

Examples:
- Saying no to an unnecessary favor
- Sharing your opinion in a group discussion
- Not letting others interrupt you
- Speaking up about microaggressions
- Asking for flexibility at work
- Tactfully addressing problematic behavior

Don't announce your intention. Just behaving assertively naturally empowers observers.

Share Your Journey

Openly discuss your process of becoming more assertive with those who know you well. Your vulnerability and growth story can inspire them.

Share:
- Situations you used to handle passively
- Fears and barriers you had to overcome
- Mindset shifts that empowered you
- Skills you had to practice
- How increased assertiveness has improved your life

Even small anecdotes demonstrating change can motivate others.

Lead Assertiveness Workshops

Volunteer to lead workshops teaching assertiveness skills at community centers, colleges, nonprofits, women's organizations or professional groups.

Topics can include:
- Overcoming limiting beliefs
- Setting boundaries
- Effective communication strategies
- Handling difficult conversations
- Advocating at work
- Managing pushback/rejection

Guiding others through curriculum solidifies your own expertise.

Form Support Groups

Start or join assertiveness focused support groups to provide community for those embarking on the journey.

Discuss:
- Celebrating small wins
- Troubleshooting setbacks
- Sharing personal experiences
- Practicing scenarios
- Exploring difficult emotions
- Supporting and motivating one another

Mutual empowerment accelerates individual growth.

Mentor Someone Directly

Take on a mentee looking to build their assertiveness and meet regularly to support their development.

Offer:
- Advice based on your experience
- Perspective on their specific challenges

- Encouraging feedback on progress
- Reminders to believe in themselves
- Help setting manageable goals
- Accountability and structure

Give the guidance you once needed to someone at an earlier phase.

Call Out Double Standards Respectfully

Challenge double standards when you observe them while maintaining composure.

Examples:

- Note when assertive women are labelled "difficult" but assertive men seen as "strong leaders."
- Question why female employees are expected to take notes while male ones contribute ideas in meetings.
- Push back against those who expect women to be deferential and passive.

Surface biases through your own example of confident advocacy.

Recognize Character Over Bravado

Praise those who display true assertiveness through respect and humility. Note people who shout loudest often lack substance.

Observe:

- Who listens well and compromises while still standing firm.
- Those able to thoughtfully disagree without ego escalating.
- Who gives credit and recognizes others' strengths.
- People with the confidence to admit when they're wrong.

Call out those embodying assertiveness positively to reinforce the right behaviors.

You have so much to offer those at earlier stages of the assertiveness journey, both through your actions and active guidance. Pay forward the wisdom you've gained. Your courage to grow reminds others growth is possible. Trust your transformation can empower countless people.

Chapter 11: Troubleshooting Setbacks

Progress toward increased assertiveness rarely follows a straight path. There are inevitable setbacks along the winding road.

When you stumble, it's important not to beat yourself up or see it as failure. Backsliding is normal. The key is examining what led to the setback, learning from it, and getting back on track.

Let's explore constructive ways to respond to common assertiveness setbacks:

Reverting to Passive Habits in Familiar Situations

Old dynamics and conditioning can pull you back into passive communication patterns with certain people or in familiar situations.

If you notice this happening:

● Pause and consciously choose a different response that aligns with your assertiveness goals.

● Reflect afterward on what triggered the regressive behavior and make an alternative plan for next time.

● Be compassionate with yourself. These associations run deep. Change takes patience.

● Consider what needs have not been addressed causing you to fall back on past coping mechanisms.

● Recommit to your assertiveness intentions going forward.

You have all the tools now. Temporary backslides help strengthen them.

Speaking Too Aggressively

There will be times when frustration leads you to express yourself too forcefully and without adequate care for the other party. Don't despair.

If this occurs:

● Take responsibility quickly and sincerely apologize for the outburst.

● Explain the context that you felt heated in the moment.

● Note your commitment to improve how you discuss issues in the future.

- Once things have settled, reflect on what triggered such an strong emotional reaction and strategize ways to better regulate in the future.
- Ask how you could have framed your viewpoint more thoughtfully.
- Thank the other person for their patience and understanding.

You can repair harm done through non-defensive accountability. Stay committed to progress.

Allowing Disrespect or Boundary Crossing

There will be times you let disrespect, microaggressions, or boundary crossing slide instead of asserting yourself in real-time. Avoid exacerbating this by:

- Accepting you missed an opportunity without spiraling into regret.
- Evaluating why you avoided speaking up and strategizing to counteract that next time.
- Having a thoughtful conversation to address the issue after the fact when possible.
- Forgiving yourself and remembering you're still learning new habits.
- Using it as a learning experience rather than proof of failure.
- Trusting you will catch more of these moments as assertiveness skills become natural.

Improvement comes through compassionate self-correction when you stumble.

Losing Your Cool in a High Stakes Situation

Big challenges will test your new assertiveness skills. Emotions may get the best of you when the stakes feel especially high. Counteract this by:

- Taking a time out to calm down after the interaction before assessing what went wrong.
- Separating your emotional reaction from your evaluation of the situation. Address the former through journaling or venting to supportive friends first.
- Once calm, look at the situation rationally. What triggered such a strong reaction? Where did you lose composure? How might you better regulate next time?

• Consider outside perspective from trusted mentors. What could you have done differently?

• Make an assertive plan for how to approach the issue next time. Visualize maintaining your cool.

With big triggers, the emotional aftermath requires as much care as the actual event. Process thoroughly.

Experiencing Imposter Syndrome

New confidence may be followed by imposter syndrome and self-doubt. Combat this by:

• Journaling about past accomplishments and examples contrary to the inner critic.

• Making a list of your capabilities, value, and positive qualities. Keep it handy when you need a reminder.

• Sharing your feelings with someone close to you. Ask for their perspective on your strengths.

• Looking objectively at tangible markers of progress, like goals met.

• Avoiding negative comparisons to others. Stay focused on your growth.

• Remembering discomfort signifies growth. The path should feel challenging.

• Trusting occasional shakiness is normal after deep lifelong conditioning. Keep going.

Your inner critic will try to distract you when you start significantly changing. Don't believe the hype.

Facing Strong Pushback

As you get better at asserting yourself, some people may intensify their resistance to losing power over you. Prepare by:

• Anticipating potential areas of pushback as you get more assertive. Mentally prepare responses in advance.

• Building your support network of those who champion your growth. Lean on them when you encounter backlash.

● Committing to consistency. People may test you to see if new boundaries waver.

● Recognizing that escalating manipulation, gaslighting or other toxic behavior signifies your progress is working.

● Staying grounded in your worthiness for equality, respect and autonomy. You owe no one subservience.

Expect resistance from those invested in the status quo. But you can weather any storm.

Setbacks on the assertiveness journey are inevitable, but also invaluable for demonstrating where more growth and practice is required. The detours and delays strengthen your resilience for the long-term. Be encouraged by progress made, learn from fumbles, get back on track, and keep becoming your highest self.

Chapter 12: Overcoming Impostor Syndrome

A common hurdle when building self-confidence and assertiveness is impostor syndrome - feeling like a fraud who doesn't deserve their success.

This chapter explores strategies for overcoming impostor syndrome on your assertiveness journey.

Common Sources

Impostor syndrome often stems from:

Childhood dynamics - Perfectionist pressures or lack of support/ affirmation can program an inner critic.

Minority status - Feeling different makes you question if you truly belong.

New challenges - Rapid increases in responsibility can outpace your confidence.

Narrow definitions of competence - Measuring ability by limited metrics discounts diverse skills.

Fear of failure - Impostor syndrome is preferable to risking confirming inadequacy.

Personality traits - High achievers and introverts frequently struggle with it.

If you understand the roots, you can counteract their residual effects.

Reframe Unhealthy Thought Patterns

Impostor syndrome fuels negative self-talk. Actively reframe critical inner voices:

Instead of:

"I'm not qualified enough yet to apply for that job."

Tell yourself: "My experience equips me for this role, even if I still have learning to do. No one starts fully prepared."

Instead of: "They're going to realize I don't know what I'm doing."

Tell yourself: "Everyone is learning on the job. I deserve to be here as much as my colleagues."

Instead of: "I just got lucky accomplishing that. I couldn't do it again."

Tell yourself: "That success was the result of hard work and ability, not just luck. I can achieve it again."

Actively argue against false mental narratives until empowering perspectives take root.

Celebrate Small Wins

To combat impostor syndrome, note evidence contradicting it:
- Times you contributed valuable expertise on a project
- Positive feedback or performance reviews
- Promotions, increased responsibility, awards
- Goals accomplished through skill and dedication
- Problems solved using your unique insight
- Instances of excelling under pressure

Collect measurable data points that confirm your competence.

Seek Outside Perspective

Trusted mentors can provide reality checks countering impostor syndrome's distortion. Ask them:
- For observations on your strengths and talent.
- To re-affirm why they believe in you.
- For feedback on your areas of expertise and unique value.
- To highlight your achievements, growth, and indicators of success.

External validation helps quiet harsh internal critics.

Focus on Fulfillment Over Accolades

Award chasers will always feel inadequate, because no matter how many accolades, it's never enough. Instead, connect to the deeper fulfillment of fulfilling work.

Ask yourself:
- How does my work help others?
- What impact am I able to make?
- How does this contribute to my purpose?

- What community does this provide?
- What meaning does this add to my life?

Impact brings longer lasting satisfaction than applause.

Remember Growth Mindset

Impostor syndrome drops you into a fixed mindset measuring yourself by static metrics. Adopt a growth mindset instead.

Remind yourself:

- Abilities can be developed with effort over time. Mastery evolves.
- Challenges are opportunities to expand your skills, not proof you lack skills.
- No one is perfect. Asking questions and making mistakes is how we learn.
- Your potential is not finite. It can keep growing through determination.

Progress requires a growth mindset undeterred by imperfections.

Make Fear Your Friend

The discomfort of impostor syndrome can motivate growth or paralysis. Make it your friend.

When you feel that discomfort:

- Recognize anxiety means you're challenging comfort zones to expand your capabilities.
- Allow the adrenaline spike to fuel your focus and determination.
- Embrace self-doubt as an invitation to gain confidence through practice.

Let impostor syndrome propel your learning, not inhibit it.

The road to overcoming impostor syndrome is committing to the journey of continually disproving it through courage, self-affirmation, and pursuing work aligned with your purpose and passions. Don't give in when the inner critic rears its head. Keep growing. You belong exactly where you are.

Adjust Perfectionist Tendencies

Perfectionism fuels impostor syndrome. Strive for excellence but remember:

- Aim for progress, not perfection. Growth requires mistakes.

- Don't equate your entire value as a person with narrow measures of achievement.
- Ask yourself what is truly "good enough" to keep moving forward. Don't get paralyzed chasing the impossible.
- Evaluate yourself on effort and intentions rather than just outcomes. Outcomes are not fully in your control.
- Progress will come through consistency, not perfection. Stay focused on the long game.

Release the need to be flawless in order to be worthy.

Leverage Testimonials

Compile testimonials and expressions of gratitude from those you've helped through your work. Re-read them when you doubt yourself.

- Performance reviews and colleague compliments
- Praise from leadership on projects
- Thank you notes from clients or customers
- Positive feedback from students/trainees
- Comments conveying the difference you made

Evidence of lives impacted through your contributions affirms your competence.

Visualize Success

Envision handling your biggest upcoming challenges smoothly and confidently. Mental rehearsal breeds real world boldness.

Before a big presentation, talk, evaluation etc. visualize:

- Speaking eloquently, making persuasive points
- Answering questions thoughtfully and thoroughly
- Staying cool and collected from start to finish
- Earning great feedback and kudos afterwards

Replace self-doubt with vivid scenes of accomplishing goals.

Emulate Positive Role Models

Note respected people you look up to who seem comfortable professionally being themselves.

Observe how they:

- Handle responsibility and pressure with grace
- Remain open to learning from others
- Discuss mistakes without defensiveness
- Own their expertise and strengths self-assuredly
- Carry themselves in alignment with their values

Model their qualities and self-confidence. Fake it till you make it.

YOU deserve to move past impostor syndrome to recognize your full talents and potential without self-doubt holding you back. Keep advocating for yourself and growing. The world needs your unique abilities.

Chapter 13: Assertiveness for Introverts

Introverts can struggle with assertiveness due to social anxiety, fear of vulnerability, and low external processing tendencies. However, assertiveness can absolutely be developed as an introvert with some adaptations.

Let's explore assertiveness strategies tailored for introverted temperaments:

Leverage Your Strengths

Introverts build confidence by spending time in their preferred environment - solitary or small group settings. Leverage these to energize:

- Spend intentional alone time to recharge before high stakes interactions.
- Process feelings and thoughts through journaling.
- Prepare mentally for challenging scenarios through visualization.
- Limit social availability to preserve energies.
- Socialize in small get togethers with close friends to build courage.

Replenish your battery through activities that feel naturally restorative.

Listen More Than You Speak

Introverts share thoughts externally through formulated internal processing. Take time to gather information before asserting your perspective:

- Ask clarifying questions to better understand the situation.
- Listen closely to others' viewpoints first. Take notes.
- Research the topic/individuals involved to get context.
- Write out your key talking points privately first.
- Speak up once you've prepared your thoughts, not impulsively.

Thoughtful input is more persuasive than hasty interjection. Wait for the right opening.

Write It Out

Writing allows you to communicate assertively in your own space. Use it to gather courage:

- Write a script to practice assertive conversations aloud solo first.

● Draft an email or letter to someone you find intimidating. Edit it to perfection before sending.

● Keep a note on your phone of concise points to share at intimidating meetings.

● Send follow up written correspondence after difficult talks to reinforce boundaries.

● Write out grievances in a letter - you can share later if appropriate.

Put your natural writing aptitude to use. Words are your friends.

Schedule Energy Drains Strategically

Manage your limited social stamina strategically by planning energy drains like conferences or big meetings when you can recharge after:

● Don't schedule anything else demanding on those days.

● Build in alone time to unwind after.

● Limit social obligations the rest of the week.

● Communicate your needs for down time to those you live with.

● Plan something enjoyable after to restore your batteries.

You'll confront challenges with greater confidence if your energy is strategically protected.

Set Boundaries Around Social Time

Prevent burnout by setting clear boundaries for your social bandwidth like:

● Needing at least 1-2 weekend days/weeknights for alone time.

● Not engaging in lengthy phone calls - prefer quick check-ins and email.

● Bringing a time limit into open ended social engagements.

● Having a set cut-off time for the day where you won't make additional plans.

● Saying no to last minute invites when you're feeling drained.

You can maintain fulfilling relationships while honoring your introverted limits.

Normalize Saying No

Introverts often acquiesce to avoid letting people down. But you aren't required to say yes to every request on your time and energy. Start building "no" into your vocabulary:

- "No, but thank you for thinking of me."
- "I can't commit to that, but appreciate the invite."
- "No, I don't have the bandwidth currently."
- "I'm not able to make it, but hope you all have a great time."
- "I'm going to have to say no to that, but let me know if there's another way I can help out."

Don't offer a litany of excuses. A simple "no" will do just fine.

If Avoiding Conflict, Address Indirectly

Introverts tend to avoid direct confrontation about issues, but bottling up your feelings hurts relationships. Address issues through:

- A thoughtful email or letter explaining your perspective.
- Asking a mediator to facilitate the dialogue.
- Meeting in a comfortable environment like over a walk rather than sitting face-to-face.
- Roleplaying the conversation aloud first to gather courage.
- Starting small with minor issues and building up towards bigger ones.

There are alternatives to aggressive confrontation. Play to your strengths.

The key is leveraging your natural introverted tendencies for preparation and deep processing to assert yourself at the right times with confidence. Give yourself space to recharge your social batteries and approach challenging situations thoughtfully in writing when possible. Remember, true assertiveness does not require extroversion - just self-advocacy.

Before major social events...

- Give yourself an overview of who will be there and key conversation topics expected. Mentally prepare.
- Arrive early to settle in without the scrutiny of a big entrance.

- Have scripts in mind for introducing yourself comfortably and exiting conversations gracefully.
- Plan an escape route - either a quiet room on site or leaving early.

Planning reduces social anxiety.

During intense meetings...

- Sit near the end of a table rather than being front and center.
- Have notes handy to glance at when you want to contribute.
- Look for opportunities to acknowledge others' good points before raising your own.
- Direct eye contact can feel intimidating - glance just above eyeline.
- Have a glass of water handy in case your voice gets shaky.

Strategic positioning and prepping your talking points helps calm nerves.

If asked a confrontational question...

- Buy time by asking them to clarify or elaborate first. Repeat their question back.
- Take a sip of water and gather your thoughts before responding. Silence is okay.
- If you're too upset to respond well, it's okay to say you need time to process and will follow up.
- Focus on resolving the issue, not attacking the person.

It's not about having an immediate smooth comeback. Thoughtful response matters more.

After tense interactions...

- Make time to be alone and decompress. Process how you feel through journaling.
- Write a revised script for how you wished you responded - practice for next time.
- Celebrate yourself for courage points - for instance, speaking up at all.

- Let go of what you cannot control - others' reactions or past events. Refocus on the next small step.

Special care is needed to recharge in solitude when tensions run high.

The key is not forcing yourself to take on extroverted tendencies. Play to your introverted strengths while finding small ways to assert your needs. With care and courage,

Before a nerve-wracking conversation...

- Write out everything you want to express. Get it all out on paper.
  - Boil it down to 3-5 key points to convey concisely.
  - Practice aloud in front of a mirror or record yourself. Refine the message.
  - Visualize the best, worst and most likely response scenarios to prepare.
  - Schedule it when you have downtime afterwards to recover.
  Meticulous preparation eases anxiety and boosts confidence.

If overwhelmed during confrontation...

- Request a short break to collect yourself privately. Splash cold water on your face.
  - Offer to resume the conversation at a specified later time when cooler heads can prevail.
  - Explain you process verbally through writing and would like to share thoughts after reflection.
  - If needed, ask a friend join for emotional support.
  - Know your limits and don't hesitate to walk away from toxic situations.
  It's okay to pump the brakes and re-center yourself before responding.

When establishing a boundary...

- Don't apologize or justify the boundary, simply state it clearly.
  - Keep verbal explanations concise. Additional detail can invite negotiation.
  - Follow up in writing to reinforce boundaries after the conversation.

● Hold your ground consistently - don't make exceptions that undermine boundaries.

● Know it's healthier to let go of people who won't respect reasonable limits.

Stick to brevity in order to maintain courage and firmness.

After an energizing group hangout...

● Build in solo downtime to recharge your social batteries.
  ● Reflect on what social interactions energized you. Do more of those.
  ● Feel proud for pushing past comfort zones, even in small ways.
  ● Write down fun memories and insights gained to look back on later.
  ● Text friends appreciation for including you.
  ● Spend time doing activities that reset and restore you.
  Leverage the motivating rush of socializing, then replenish.

Assertiveness as an introvert requires strategizing around your natural inclinations - but done with care for your needs, it can absolutely be achieved. Be proud of each small step forward!

Chapter 14: Assertiveness in Romantic Relationships

Romantic relationships offer fertile ground for practicing assertive communication skills. Navigating vulnerability, conflict, and compromise with a partner allows you to articulate your needs, boundaries, and perspective in an intimate setting.

While all relationships require compromise, you should not have to sacrifice your core values, deal breakers, and emotional needs to sustain the connection long-term.

Let's explore assertiveness strategies to build healthy romantic relationships:

Set Expectations Early On

Have an open discussion early in dating around core values, goals, communication styles, emotional needs, and relationship deal breakers.

Address:

• Temperament compatibility - introvert vs extrovert, planning vs spontaneity etc.
• Love languages - physical touch, quality time, words of affirmation etc.
• Ideal frequency for seeing each other and future living preferences
• Faith, politics, culture - any differences to discuss
• Communication and conflict resolution styles
• Past relationship patterns - lessons learned

Getting aligned from the start prevents misunderstandings down the line. Be honest about who you are and what you need.

Speak Up About Grievances

Don't let minor grievances bottle up through avoiding difficult discussions. Voice hurt feelings or frustrations early and thoughtfully:

• Set a time to chat where you can both listen without distractions.

- Use "I feel" language rather than accusations. Explain how the issue makes you feel.
- After sharing your perspective, allow them space to explain theirs.
- Brainstorm solutions together. Compromise where possible.
- Thank them for hearing you out and reaffirm your care for them.

Hashing out little issues early prevents major blow ups later.

Negotiate Needs

Openly discuss your needs and differences in preferences early on, like personal space, socializing, affection, words of affirmation etc.

- Don't present your needs as right and theirs as wrong - frame them as differences to bridge.
- Identify areas of flexibility and compromise.
- Discuss strategies to ensure both feel cared for.
- Agree on a trial period to test compromises and re-evaluate after.
- Check-in regularly on fulfillment of mutual needs. Make adjustments as required.

Compromise should make both people feel considered, not one side engulfed.

Set Boundaries Respectfully

Everyone has reasonable boundaries. Communicate yours clearly and stick to them consistently.

Examples include:
- How much personal space/alone time you need
- Your boundaries on flirting with others
- What you are willing to share financially
- Your sexual boundaries
- How much time you'll spend with their friends/family

A respectful partner may be disappointed by a boundary but will understand and comply rather than pressure, guilt trip, or retaliate.

Don't Lose Your Sense of Self

Amid the intimacy and compromise of relationships, maintain a grounded sense of your identity.

- Regularly do activities that connect you to your core self.
- Surround yourself with people who know and love you as you.
- Discuss any concerns about losing yourself in the relationship.
- If walking on eggshells, evaluate dynamics. You should feel free to be you.

Bring your best self to the relationship by nurturing your solo development.

Request Support Around Growth Areas

We all have areas for emotional growth. Ask directly for support around vulnerabilities, sensitivities, toxic patterns etc.

Examples:

- "I tend to get defensive when criticized due to childhood dynamics. Please be patient with me as I work on that."
- "When you dismiss plans last minute, I feel abandoned due to past experiences. Can you reassure me when that happens?"

Asking for support cultivates intimacy. But also assess if fundamental incompatibilities exist.

Discuss Relationship Growth

Check in regularly about what's going well in the relationship and goals for continued growth like:

- Travel plans, big purchases, future vision
- Strengthening intimacy, trust, connection
- Resolving lingering irritations before they widen
- Improving communication around needs
- Ideas for supporting each other's personal growth

Relationships shouldn't plateau. Keep investing through open dialogue.

Being assertive involves advocating your boundaries unapologetically while also caring deeply for your partner's fulfillment. Share your authentic self and needs while also compromising considerably. With commitment, assertive communication breeds security and guides the relationship to deeper intimacy.

Don't hint - be direct

Passive aggressive hints invite misunderstanding and breed resentment. Clearly state your thoughts, needs, and concerns directly but compassionately.

Avoid:
- "It's fine if you want to cancel our plans again."
- "I don't mind if you forgot my birthday."

Do say:
- "I feel hurt when you cancel our plans last minute."
- "It's important to me that we celebrate birthdays."

Take the guesswork out of important conversations.

Appreciate efforts

If your partner makes genuine efforts to meet your needs better after you've asserted them, express sincere appreciation.

For example:
- "Thank you for being more conscious about responding when I open up."
- "I notice you've really made an effort to keep our weekends free like we discussed and I want you to know I appreciate it."

Positive reinforcement motivates continued progress.

Own your feelings

Avoid blaming language like "You're making me feel..." when expressing emotions. Own your feelings using "I" statements:

Instead of: "You're making me feel neglected."

Say: "I've been feeling somewhat neglected since we haven't had much quality time lately."

This invites problem solving, not defensiveness.

Don't stew - speak up

Assertiveness means addressing issues early before resentment silently builds. If something bothers you, don't stew - speak up respectfully right away, before a little thing becomes a big thing.

Adapt your approach

We relate to different people differently. Reflect on how your partner best receives difficult feedback, and tailor your assertive communication accordingly.

With practice, assertiveness in romantic relationships becomes second nature. Don't lose yourself or neglect emotional needs. You deserve mutual fulfillment, understanding and respect.

Copy

Continue

N

Here are some additional assertive communication tips for romantic relationships:

Don't be a mind reader

Don't expect your partner to automatically know your needs and preferences. Clearly and proactively express them.

If you need:

- More quality time together, request specific date ideas.
- More words of affirmation, share how much that means to you.
- More physical affection, discuss how to mutually meet that need.

Assertiveness means taking responsibility for voicing your needs instead of silently expecting your partner to intuit them.

Learn each other's triggers

Pay attention to when and why communication tends to break down. Understanding each other's triggers helps avoid or thoughtfully navigate them.

For example:

- If one partner grew up in a passive aggressive family, hints and sarcasm can quickly escalate tension.
- If one values blunt honesty and the other gentler feedback, tone and phrasing requires care.

Figuring out each other's sensitivities and hot buttons enables handling them with compassion.

Discuss preferred conflict resolution styles

Everyone handles disagreement differently. Discuss your conflict styles:

- Does one person need to cool off while the other craves immediate resolution?
- Does one obsessively analyze issues while the other wants to move on quickly?

Understanding these differences allows you to navigate conflicts in ways that make both partners feel heard and respected.

Observe non-verbal cues

Don't just listen to your partner's words. Note their body language and tone. If non-verbals conflict with their words, gently check in on how they really feel.

Listening with your eyes as well as ears strengthens intuitive understanding.

Healthy assertiveness means speaking your truth while also caring deeply about your partner's happiness and perspective. With mutual empathy, compromise and emotional intelligence, assertive communication builds secure, lasting love.

Don't avoid the DTR (Define The Relationship) talk

It's easy to let the relationship drift along without clear expectations. But ambiguity breeds insecurity. Initiate an open discussion to get on the same page about:

- Short and long term relationship goals
- Mutual desires and expectations
- Boundaries around intimacy and faithfulness
- How you want to present your relationship publicly
- Any differences requiring compromise

You'll both feel more secure with defined expectations.

Discuss love languages

Everyone expresses and feels loved in different ways. Discuss your love languages and how to fill each other's emotional "tanks":

- Words of affirmation
- Quality time
- Physical touch
- Acts of service
- Gift giving

Understanding love languages allows you to communicate care effectively.

Check your narratives

Don't impose past relationship patterns or prototypes onto your partner. Check assumptions through open dialogue:

- Avoid statements like "You're just like my ex who..."
- Discuss differences between this relationship and past ones.
- Don't catastrophize occasional issues as doomed patterns.
- Rewrite negative narratives you place on relationships.

Stay present rather than projecting fears onto your partner.

Address mental load imbalances

Many relationships fall into dynamics where one partner carries the mental load of managing the household and relationship tasks. Discuss this openly. Make conscious efforts to balance it.

Healthy long-term love requires assertive communication, emotional intelligence, mutual empathy, and perseverance.

Chapter 15: Standing Up to Manipulation

As you become more assertive, manipulative people may intensify their passive aggressive tactics to regain control over you.

Manipulators use guilt, uncertainty, obligation and other psychological tactics to influence you against your best interests. Learning to recognize and stand up to manipulation is key for maintaining assertiveness.

Let's explore how to assert boundaries against common manipulation techniques:

Guilt Tripping

Manipulators make you feel guilty for imposing on them or not meeting their needs. Respond by:

● Acknowledging they feel upset without conceding guilt. "I understand you feel hurt that I can't attend."

● Broken record technique - calmly repeat your stance. "I wish I could be there, but I already have plans and won't be able to change them."

● Recommend solutions that don't require your sacrifice. "I'm happy to celebrate another time that works for both of us."

● Note by respecting your own needs, you're modelling healthy behavior for the relationship.

Stay empathetic but refuse to absorb misplaced guilt. The feeling should lead to growth, not appeasement.

Passive Aggressiveness

Passive aggression punishes through indirect resistance instead of direct conflict. Combat it by:

● Asking clarifying questions to get to the true concern. "It seems like there might be something else frustrating you. I'd like to understand."

● Naming the dynamic directly but non-confrontationally. "I don't want unresolved feelings to negatively impact our relationship. Let's discuss this openly."

● Suggesting a time-out if tensions escalate to revisit the talk later calmly.

● Modeling open communication. "In the future I hope we can address problems directly instead of through passive aggression."

Keep dialogue thoughtful but uncompromising. Passive aggression derails healthy relating.

Projecting Blame

Manipulators deflect accountability by painting themselves as victims and blaming you as the aggressor. Counter this by:

● Acknowledging context but re-focusing the discussion on their actions, not general circumstances. "I understand your workload is heavy, but I'd like to discuss my concerns about how it impacted me."

● Affirming their emotions while clarifying intent. "I know you feel attacked, but my goal is to resolve this, not lay blame."

● Extracting concrete agreements on behavioral changes, not just apologies.

The blame game distracts from productive conflict resolution. Refocus the conversation on mutual understanding.

Catastrophizing

Painting reasonable boundaries or feedback dramatically leads to you consoling them. Recognize catastrophizing and re-center the discussion:

● Emphasize this isn't the end of the relationship, just a specific issue to work through.

● Validate emotions without ceding on your boundaries. "I know you're upset, but I still need __ to feel comfortable."

● Repeat your stance calmly without getting defensive or escalating emotions.

● Suggest speaking later when cooler heads may prevail.

You can empathize while still holding your ground. Their emotions shouldn't deter your boundaries.

Emotional Blackmail

Threatening self-harm if demands aren't met is severe emotional blackmail. Handle it by:

- Clearly stating you refuse to be manipulated but are happy to get them professional help.
- Following through on setting the boundary for both your well-beings.
- Only providing reassurance that aligns with your values and priorities.
- Escaping if ever physically threatened or endangered.

Your health and safety come first. You are not responsible for others' destructive choices. Seek outside support if needed.

Standing up to manipulation keeps your integrity and emotional health intact. Remember:

- You teach people how to treat you. Demand respectful communication.
- Progress may require letting go of manipulative relationships for your own well-being.
- There is no winning with manipulators. The only way forward is maintaining your boundaries confidently.

You've got this. Assert your right to be treated with dignity while also maintaining self-control and compassion. Keep taking the high road.

Broken record technique

Manipulators will try to wear you down and argue endlessly to get their way. Stay strong by calmly repeating your stance like a broken record:

"I understand you want me to ___, but I will not be able to do that."

Don't get sucked into endless back and forth. Firmly but compassionately repeat your decision.

Set consequences

Boundaries without consequences get crossed. Make clear the consequences if they continue to ignore your boundaries.

For example:

"If you show up unannounced again after we have discussed this, I will have to reconsider our living arrangement."

Be prepared to follow through on proportional consequences when they test your resolve.

Limit information sharing

The less manipulators know, the less they can use against you. Share minimally when dealing with toxic people prone to triangulation, gossip, or smear campaigns.

Information is power. Don't hand them ammunition to manipulate you or distort facts. Keep communication brief, direct and superficial.

Seek outside perspective

Manipulators try isolating you and making you question your own judgment. Check in with trusted friends to maintain perspective.

Ask if they've noticed controlling behavior or patterns of manipulation in this relationship. Listen to their impartial feedback.

Document incidents

Keep a record of boundary violations, agreements broken, and other manipulative behaviors.

Documentation helps:
- Identify patterns of manipulation over time
- Reference details accurately when incidents get distorted
- Review if questioning your judgment

Trust tangible evidence over gaslighting and denial.

Guard your mind and heart against manipulation through calm vigilance. You deserve relationships built on mutual care, not control.

Don't justify or explain excessively

Manipulators leverage information you share and scramble your boundaries. Set limits through unambiguous statements rather than lengthy explanations.

Instead of:

"You've been pressuring me a lot about this lately and it's making me really uncomfortable. Given our history together, I know your intentions are good, but I really need to focus on myself right now..."

Say:

"I won't be able to do that. Please do not ask me again."

Simple, direct communication leaves little opening for debate.

Watch out for false apologies

Beware apologies that sound insincere or come with strings attached. Real change requires accountability and altered behavior over time.

For example:

"I'm sorry you feel that way." "I'm sorry, but I was just trying to help you see..."

These excuses shift blame rather than taking real ownership. Don't settle for empty apologies. Wait and observe their behavioral changes.

Grey rock method

When engaging with known manipulators, become as boring and non-reactive as a grey rock to discourage emotional hooks.

Give bland, superficial responses. Share nothing personal. Change topics away from anything controversial. Disengage as soon as possible.

Don't feed their drama.

Strategic silence

When manipulators try pushing your buttons, sometimes the strongest response is no response.

Silence paired with unwavering boundaries speaks volumes. Don't give them the fight or tearful reaction they want.

Calmly reiterate your stance, then disengage. Silence destabilizes manipulators.

Trust your gut and stand your ground against manipulation. You deserve healthy relationships with equal partners, not control.

Don't be derailed by deflection

When confronting a manipulator about their behavior, they may try to derail the conversation by suddenly bringing up a past mistake of yours.

Refocus the discussion:

"I want to have a productive dialogue with you, but first I'd like to resolve the issue I originally raised."

Don't take the bait of getting sidetracked.

Leave the door open to positive change

While maintaining firm boundaries, leave room for the possibility of eventual sincere change.

Phrase boundaries like:

"Unless/until I see..." "Moving forward, I need..."

This upholds your standards while allowing hope for growth if they confront unhealthy patterns.

Seek validation from safe people

If you've been conditioned by a manipulator to ignore your needs, reconnect with emotionally safe friends to regain perspective.

Ask if they've noticed controlling behavior you may have become desensitized to. Listen with an open mind even if it's hard to hear.

Set relationship dealbreakers

Decide what behaviors would necessitate ending the relationship for your well-being, like:

- Physical intimidation
- Repeated boundary violations
- Sudden anger outbursts
- Pathological lying
- Emotional abuse

Know your dealbreakers so you don't endure unacceptable treatment.

Limit time together

Interactions with manipulative people can quickly turn draining. Limit exposure:

- Keep visits brief
- Only meet in public places
- Block them digitally during vulnerable times
- Schedule mandatory self-care after engagements

Manage your energy. You come first.

Staying assertive against manipulation helps protect your emotional health and relationships.

Chapter 16: Assertiveness for Anxious People

Many who struggle with assertiveness also wrestle with social anxiety, fear of judgment, and discomfort being the center of attention. Their anxious tendencies can make speaking up feel terrifying.

However, there are effective strategies to build assertiveness skills even for those prone to anxiety. With preparation and practice, you can express your needs and boundaries in spite of nervousness.

Let's explore techniques to help anxious people strengthen assertiveness:

Start Small to Build Confidence

Don't begin by confronting your biggest fears. Start with low-stakes situations to gain confidence in your skills before working up to more anxiety-provoking ones.

Easy starter steps:
- Asserting preferences to a server at a restaurant
- Asking for clarification of instructions from a supportive person
- Sharing your opinion in a casual online forum
- Saying no to a favor from a friend if you're too busy
- Pointing out a minor grievance politely

Check small successes off your list to motivate taking bigger risks in time.

Rehearse Scenarios in Advance

The unknown breeds anxiety. Thoroughly plan assertive responses to probable scenarios ahead of time.

- Script out what you want to express and practice aloud.
- Anticipate possible reactions or curveballs and decide your response.
- Record yourself and refine until it feels natural.
- Visualize handling challenging moments smoothly.

Meticulous preparation and rehearsal eases nerves and boosts confidence.

Lean Into Discomfort Strategically

Accept that assertiveness will feel uncomfortable at first. Lean into small doses of anxiety intentionally to build tolerance like:
- Making slightly bolder requests or refusals each week
- Sharing one new viewpoint or perspective weekly
- Regularly asking someone clarifying questions
- Practicing eye contact and open body language when anxious
- Role playing feared scenarios with a friend

Desensitize yourself to discomfort gradually. It gets easier.

Structure Unpredictable Situations

Create more certainty around unpredictable interactions making you anxious. Strategies include:
- Asking to receive meeting agendas and prep materials in advance
- Arriving early to set up seats on the less anxiety-provoking side of a room
- Having scripts handy to guide high stakes conversations
- Scheduling timed breaks to re-center yourself when overwhelmed
- Focusing on deep breathing when you feel anxiety spike

Insert structure and breathing room to limit uncertainty.

Reframe Perfectionistic Thoughts

Anxious people often obsess over doing things perfectly. Curb this by reframing:
- "Mistakes mean I'm learning."
- "Progress requires messiness."
- "What's the minimal viable step I can take?"
- "My worth isn't defined by outcomes."
- "I want to avoid regrets more than mistakes."

Strive for growth over perfection so fear doesn't paralyze you.

Create a Calming Environment

Surround yourself with relaxing sensory elements to lower anxiety.

Ideas:

- Play calming music or nature sounds
- Display artwork or photos eliciting happy memories
- Keep cozy blankets available to bundle up in
- Infuse relaxing essential oil scents
- Limit clutter and stimulus to create peaceful spaces

Let your environment help counterbalance inner frenzy.

Reframe Nervousness as Excitement

Reframe anxiety as energizing, not debilitating. Nervousness often manifests physically identically to excitement.

When you feel anxious:

- Recognize it as arousal pumping you up, not weakening you.
- Mentally relabel it "excitement" and channel it into passion.
- Use the adrenaline spike to fuel determined focus.
- Take deep power breaths rather than panicked shallow ones.

Harness the rush to embolden instead of inhibit you.

Celebrate Small Courageous Steps

Praise yourself for any act of assertiveness, no matter how minor it may seem objectively. Anxiety makes each one feel like a huge accomplishment.

- Note it in a victory journal to review and motivate you during setbacks.
- Tell a supportive friend who will cheer you on.
- Give yourself a small reward like watching your favorite show after.
- Savor the progress and remember each win builds your confidence.

With compassionate patience for the process, you can develop assertiveness skills despite anxiety and gain control over fear rather than allowing fear to control you.

If you feel a panic attack coming on...

- Name it - "I'm having a panic attack but this too shall pass." Calling it out can help diffuse it.

- Focus on slow, deep belly breathing rather than short, shallow chest breathing during panic attacks.
- Splash cool water on your face or hold an ice cube. The temperature shock can help snap you out of mounting anxiety.
- Visualize your happy place - a peaceful scene that brings joy and calm.
- Play calming music and engage your senses - the smells, sounds, textures around you.

Grounding yourself in the present helps prevent anxiety spiraling.

When asserting yourself, speak slowly

Fast talking often signals nervousness while slow, purposeful speech conveys confidence.

Concentrate on slowing your rate of speech. Pause between sentences to breathe.

This calms you while also commanding greater presence.

Channel nervous energy productively

Rather than waiting anxiously before a stressful situation, purposely channel that energy:

- Clean or organize your space
- Go for a jog or do push ups to release adrenaline
- Immerse yourself in a distracting activity like a puzzle
- Practice your assertive talking points aloud

Expending nervous energy in constructive ways helps take the edge off anxiety.

Approach new people at social events

Rather than waiting anxiously for people to approach you, take small risks like:

- Smiling warmly as you pass people and saying hello
- Giving a sincere compliment on something you admire about someone
- Introducing yourself briefly to start safe small talk

Approaching others first eases social anxiety over time.

Remember: most people are anxious too

Social anxiety makes us feel like the only awkward person in the room. But the reality is most people feel insecurity and are too focused on themselves to closely judge you.

Knowing that everyone feels nervous and insecure paradoxically calms your own social anxiety. We're all in this together.

With compassionate patience in the process, assertiveness can absolutely be learned, even if anxiety creates bumps along the way. Keep celebrating small wins!

Set a time limit for worrying

It's easy for anxious minds to endlessly obsess over possible worst case scenarios. Ease this by setting a timer for a short time limit for worrying - say 5-10 minutes. When it goes off, consciously shift your focus onto something constructive.

Ask loved ones for encouragement

Let close friends/family know you're working on being more assertive and will likely need extra encouragement. Ask them to remind you of your capabilities and progress when you struggle with self-doubt.

Avoid reassurance seeking from critical people

The validation of those who undermine your confidence brings temporary relief but long term self-doubt. Instead, seek reassurance only from safe supporters.

After anxiety-provoking interactions...

- Make note of what went well, not just what didn't. Find the learning.
  - Jot down what new fears you confronted and how you stayed resilient.
  - Text a friend something you feel proud of, however small.
  - Write a list of your strengths and past successes.

- Remind yourself that courage requires facing fear.

Reflect on wins, not just shortcomings. Be your own cheerleader.

Before anxiety-provoking events...

- Do light exercise to discharge nervous energy.
  - Listen to motivational music with empowering lyrics.
  - Review your skills and qualifications relevant to the situation.
  - Visualize handling it successfully. Picture yourself feeling proud after.
  - Affirm that you've grown beyond old limits.

Priming your mindset for success gives confidence a head start over anxiety.

Have compassion for yourself and celebrate every act of courage, no matter how small it may seem. With time and commitment, assertive habits will grow stronger than anxious tendencies. You've got this!

Chapter 17: Developing Assertiveness as an Empath

When you are naturally empathetic and attuned to others' emotions, assertiveness can feel especially challenging. You may struggle to set boundaries or have tough conversations out of fear of upsetting someone.

However, when done thoughtfully, assertiveness and empathy can complement one another. Setting limits while also deeply caring about others' feelings is possible with the right approach.

Let's explore strategies to develop assertiveness as a highly empathetic person:

Check Motivations

Empaths often acquiesce due to unconsciously absorbing others' emotions rather than their own authentic motivations.

Before automatically saying yes or softening feedback, pause and check in with yourself:

- Are these my true feelings or am I taking on their pain?
- Am I trying to prevent feeling their hurt rather than acting from my values?
- Would setting this limit align with my core needs and priorities?
- Is my desire to appease them at my own expense driven by my empathetic nature?

Get grounded in your own emotional boundaries first before responding. Your feelings matter too.

Set Time Limits on Support

As an empath, you likely don't want to abandon people in need. However, you also can't be endlessly drained.

Set time boundaries around support efforts:

- "I'm happy to listen for 20 minutes, but then I'll need to redirect our conversation."

● Schedule focused quality time with struggling loved ones, then limit daily check-ins.

● Establish how often and for how long you're available to offer counsel.

● Recommend professional help if issues require more support than you can sustainably provide.

You can care deeply and still have limits. Give fully during selected windows of time, then disconnect.

Limit Exposure to Highly Negative People

Extremely hostile or aggressive people quickly deplete empathic people. Minimize contact where possible:

● Keep conversations superficial to avoid energy depletion.

● Refuse to engage with them when you're already feeling overwhelmed.

● Surround yourself with positive people to recharge after exposure to negativity.

● Set firm boundaries around how often and under what conditions you'll engage.

● Give yourself permission to walk away from toxic relationships.

You deserve to protect your energy. Don't let it be hijacked.

Reframe Guilt and Worry

Empaths tend to feel guilty and worried about others' struggles even when separate from them. Counter this through reframing:

● "I trust they have inner resources to handle challenges, as I do."

● "We each walk our own path at our own pace."

● "My well-being enables me to support them best."

● "I offer guidance when I can, but cannot control outcomes."

● "I can hold space for their process without taking it on."

Have faith in others' capacity for resilience. Don't let empathy become enmeshment.

Set Reciprocity Expectations

Empaths give endlessly often without requiring reciprocation. But you deserve mutuality.

Calmly communicate:

- "I'm happy to be there for you when I'm able, but I have limits too."
- "Support has to flow both ways in close relationships."
- "My needs matter too. Can we find a way to support each other?"

Don't allow your giving nature to be exploited through one-sided dynamics. Consider whether reciprocation is present before giving more.

Learn to Say "No"

The most empathetic people struggle to say no when asked for help. Remember that setting boundaries allows you to sustainably help others long-term.

Practice saying:

- "I'm at capacity currently. I need to prioritize self-care right now."
- "I can't take that on, but let me know how else I could support you."
- "I don't have availability to help out. Can we connect another time when I may be able to assist?"

You can acknowledge their need, while still asserting your own limitations. Don't run your tank dry.

The key is realizing your sensitivity is a gift, but can become a burden without healthy boundaries. Prioritize recalibrating your own emotional equilibrium. Then you can truly listen, support, and relate to others from a grounded place.

Stay present to others' pain, but don't absorb it as your own. With practice, assertiveness and empathy can powerfully complement one another in your relationships. You've got this!

Learn to detach emotionally

Empaths tend to feel others' emotions intensely as if they were your own. When you notice this enmeshment happening:

- Mentally take a step back and remind yourself you are separate people.
- Visualize your emotional space as clearly distinct from theirs.

- Release the absorbed emotions through meditation, journaling or talking it out with other empaths.
- Affirm "These feelings belong to them, not me. I can empathize but don't need to take this on."

Conscious detachment preserves your emotional autonomy.

Set conversation time limits

It's easy to get sucked into providing unlimited counsel and reassurance to struggling people. Manage this by:

- Letting them know kindly upfront that you have limited time to talk.
- When time is winding down, let them know you need to wrap up soon.
- Schedule future follow up conversations at designated times, rather than endless venting.
- Suggest solutions like counseling so they have additional support outlets.

You can care deeply about their well-being while also maintaining healthy boundaries.

Strengthen your resilience

Make a habit of self-care practices that build your resilience as an empath like:

- Spending time alone to recharge in nature
- Creating physical and emotional space from others' energy
- Purging negative emotions through writing or art
- Replenishing your spirit through activities that spark joy
- Surrounding yourself with positive affirming people

You can't pour from an empty cup. Prioritizing your own needs enables you to empathize without depleting yourself long-term.

Set clear expectations around reciprocity

Don't wait until you're depleted to communicate your need for mutual support. Kindly but directly:

- Discuss your expectations of give and take in close relationships.
- Make requests - ask for specific caring gestures you need.

- Note when you feel your giving exceeds receiving.
- Prioritize relationships where your caring is reciprocated.

You deserve to receive nurturing too.

With practice, you can maintain an empathetic spirit while also setting the boundaries required to protect your energy and well-being. You've got this!

Chapter 18: Developing Assertiveness in Friendships

Friendships are fertile ground for practicing assertive communication skills. While it may feel uncomfortable confronting friends at first, clear self-expression deepens trust and understanding over time.

Let's explore strategies for building greater assertiveness in your friendships:

Don't Let Things Build Up

It's tempting to swallow small grievances to keep the friendship harmonious. But unaddressed irritations bottle up and turn into simmering resentment.

Speak up tactfully when something bothers you - the sooner the better. Examples:

- "I want to mention this now so it doesn't turn into a bigger deal down the road..."
- "Something has been on my mind lately, and I'd like to talk through it..."
- "I'm sure you didn't realize it bugged me, but I want to share my perspective..."

Hashing out little issues early prevents explosive confrontations later.

Don't Hint - Be Direct

It's easy to make passive aggressive hints about your hurt feelings rather than directly but compassionately expressing them. But hints breed confusion and mistrust.

Avoid:
- Giving your friend the cold shoulder without explanation
- Making snide remarks hoping they'll get the message
- Venting to others about your friend instead of the source

Do:
- Schedule a calm discussion and clearly but kindly share your viewpoint.
- Use "I feel..." language to take ownership of your emotions.

- After expressing your perspective, allow them space to explain theirs.
- Brainstorm mutual solutions.

Direct, open communication enhances intimacy. subsurface hints corrode it over time.

Set and Enforce Boundaries

You shouldn't have to fully bend your boundaries to maintain a friendship. Communicate limits clearly:

- How often you're available to talk or get together based on your capacity.
- Topics of conversation you want to avoid.
- Ways of interacting that make you uncomfortable.
- Loan terms, if willing to lend money.

Kindly but firmly hold people to respecting your stated boundaries. Don't compromise your emotional health.

Discuss Differences Openly

Pretending you see eye-to-eye on fundamental values and priorities can only last so long. Have courageous discussions around differences like:

- Parenting approaches if one of you has kids.
- Faith/cultural worldview if you have conflicting perspectives.
- Political viewpoints. Agree to keep dialogue thoughtful and avoid personal attacks.
- Social needs, if one is highly extroverted and the other more introverted.

Airing differences openly relieves secret tensions and prevents unspoken resentment.

Call Out Toxic Friend Dynamics

You deserve friends who make you feel energized, respected, and seen. Identify and limit draining friendships displaying:

- Self-centeredness or lack of interest in your life.
- Competitiveness or judgment rather than support.
- Jealousy or sabotage.

- Chronic, one-sided venting.

Initiate direct conversations to improve dynamics. But feel empowered to let go of one-way relationships.

Make Time for Friends

It's easy to get so absorbed in responsibilities you neglect friend connections. But those bonds nourish you.

Strategically prioritize nourishing friendships:

- Put social time on your calendar first, then schedule obligations around it.
- Coordinate regular video calls to catch up one-on-one.
- Alternate hosting get-togethers with different friends.
- Travel to visit long-distance friends when possible.
- Make time for friends while pursuing other goals - don't put happiness on hold.

Foster your friendships as actively as you do other priorities. Your whole life will flourish.

Developing assertiveness in your friendships builds intimacy, prevents simmering resentment, resolves differences, and makes space for each person's needs. With courage and care, you'll take your connections to beautiful new depths.

Don't be afraid to outgrow relationships

Some friendships thrive through seasons of life, then naturally fade as you change and grow apart. That's okay. Don't cling to one-sided relationships out of guilt. Politely:

- Express appreciation for the meaningful role they played previously.
- Note your priorities and needs have shifted over time.
- Suggest meeting up periodically rather than forcing constant contact.
- Loosen expectations around frequency of communication.
- Gradually let go without burning bridges.

You can treasure past connection while also acknowledging when it's time to move forward.

Address recurring bad habits upfront

If a friend has a habit that seriously bothers you like chronically being late, initiate an assertive but caring dialogue:

- Don't attack their character, frame it as an issue to solve together.
- Explain how the behavior makes you feel using "I" statements.
- Suggest solutions like agreed upon consequences or supports to improve.
- Be prepared to enforce boundaries like leaving if they're very late.
- Focus on mutual understanding.

Bad habits often persist simply because no one speaks up. Kindly express that their behavior matters to you.

Don't participate in gossip

If friends try engaging you in spreading rumors or put-downs of absent people:

- Decline to participate. Note gossip ultimately hurts relationships.
- Suggest changing the subject to more positive topics.
- If they won't move on, excuse yourself from the conversation.
- Hold them accountable if they gossip about you.
- Ultimately, limit time with untrustworthy friends.

You don't have to laugh along or stay silent. Take a stand against pettiness.

Healthy assertive relating allows you to deepen mutual support, understanding, and care with friends while also establishing necessary boundaries. You've got this!

Discuss expectations around accountability

If a friend consistently disappoints or takes your generosity for granted, have an accountability discussion:

- Review examples where you felt let down or taken advantage of.
- Ask how they think the situation could have been handled better.
- Express appreciation for any ownership they take.
- Calmly explain consequences if the pattern continues.
- Give them opportunities to rebuild trust through improved behavior.

Accountability helps friends mature the relationship.

Don't be afraid to renegotiate aspects of friendship

It's healthy for friends to reassess expectations as life situations change. Initiate dialogues about evolving needs openly and without judgment. For example:

- If you have kids, explain your changing capacity for late nights out.
- If going through grief, share your temporary need for additional support.
- If finances change, reframe your ability to split costs 50/50.

Renegotiating aspects of friendship with care deepens mutual understanding.

Share your process of growth

Choosing vulnerability helps others relate and grow. Open up about your journey:

- Share an area you're working to improve and ask their support.
- Bond over mutual struggles like dating woes, work stress, or family issues.
- Open up about insecurities, not just achievements.
- Ask for their wisdom around issues you're grappling with.

Mutual openness cements intimacy.

Healthy assertiveness balanced with care makes friendships fulfilling for all parties long-term. You've got this!

Don't compare friendships

Refrain from comparisons like "You make more effort for her than me." These often stem from jealousy rather than reality. Accept that friends show care in different ways.

Focus on whether your core needs are met in the friendship, not if it looks the same as others' relationships.

Address decreasing investment

If you've noticed a friend pulling away or putting in less effort, communicate openly:

- Share you've felt disconnected and would like to understand why.
- Ask if they're going through anything impacting the friendship.

- Suggest spending intentional quality time to reconnect.
- If necessary, mutually loosen expectations to sustain the friendship long-term.

A drifting friend may be unaware of the distance growing. Speaking up can spark re-investment.

Don't end friendships via ghosting

Abruptly cutting contact leaves no closure. If a toxic dynamic can't be resolved, have one final assertive conversation:

- Explain you value their friendship but are struggling with aspect X.
- Note what you've done to address the issue and improve the dynamic.
- Share that without change, you don't see the relationship working long-term.
- Offer to politely transition to a casual acquaintance relationship if needed.

One last direct attempt at resolution is respectful, even if the friendship must end.

Learn to forgive

Even close friends hurt each other occasionally. Assertiveness involves forgiveness when warranted:

- Note their remorse and commitment to improvement.
- Remember times you were forgiven.
- Release the urge to shame or punish.
- Repair trust gradually through demonstrated change.

With empathy and honesty, many friendships can heal and grow after injuries.

Chapter 19: Cultivating Assertive Body Language

Your body language impacts how your assertive communication is received. Adopting confident, open postures reinforces your messages visually.

Let's review assertive body language tips to practice in conversations, meetings, and confrontations:

Maintain Strong Posture

Slouching or collapsing in on yourself projects passivity and self-doubt. Stand and sit tall to convey confidence.

Tips:
- Keep your back straight, shoulders back.
- Lift your chin slightly and relax your arms.
- Take up space comfortably without stiffening up.
- Avoid crossed arms, tapping feet, or nervous fidgeting.

Proper posture communicates you believe you deserve to be heard.

Establish Comfortable Eye Contact

Looking down or avoiding eye contact suggests discomfort asserting yourself. Meet gazes directly but naturally.

Strategies:
- During conversations, briefly lock eyes, then glance away intermittently.
- Focus on eye color instead of assessing reactions.
- If sustained eye contact makes you nervous, gaze just above the eyes instead.
- Briefly break contact while speaking to gather thoughts or reference notes.

Eye contact shows engagement and confidence without intimidating.

Use Intentional Gestures

Gestures reinforce your verbal statements subtly. Use them intentionally, not nervously.

Examples:
- Open palm gestures to signal receptiveness
- Raising one finger to emphasize a key point
- Leaning in slightly when engaged, back when skeptical
- Nodding along to show understanding

Gestures make communication feel more dynamic and natural.

Convey Vocal Confidence

Your tone, volume, cadence etc. impact how your message is received. Speak clearly and deliberately.

Guidelines:
- Modulate volume appropriately without raising your voice in anger.
- Vary vocal inflection to avoid monotone and convey emphasis.
- Pause between statements rather than rushing your words.
- Fill silent spaces thoughtfully rather than nervously babbling.

Steady, grounded vocal tones project confidence and capability.

Adapt Your Body Language Culturally

Body language has cultural nuances. Adjust accordingly:
- In Asian cultures, avoid putting hands on hips and excessive gestures.
- In Latin America, standing closer is normal but avoid pats on the back.
- In Middle Eastern cultures, don't use your left hand or point your feet at others.
- With Americans, abundant eye contact conveys confidence.

When in doubt, observe local body language norms. Adapt respectfully.

Convey Assertiveness Seated

You can demonstrate confidence seated through strategies like:
- Sitting straight with feet grounded rather than crossed.

- Placing hands in lap or on armrests rather than nervously tapping.
- Leaning forward engagedly when listening rather than slouching.
- Using intentional gestures like tilting your head thoughtfully.

Mindful movements and demeanor project confidence beyond just standing postures.

Practice Regularly to Make Natural

Improving body language requires undoing years of habits. Practice regularly until assertive postures feel natural.

Ways to practice:

- Observe body language you admire in peers and mentors. Model their behaviors.
- Do regular check-ins during interactions. Are your muscles relaxed? How is your breathing?
- Ask trusted friends for body language feedback.
- Video chat yourself to analyze and adjust.
- Visualize handling stressful situations with confident body language.

With consistency, assertive physical presence will become second nature.

The next time you want to highlight an important point, make steady eye contact. Before a nerve-wracking presentation, stand tall with your shoulders back. Little movements build your assertive presence significantly over time. You've got this!

Claim your physical space

Rather than collapsing in on yourself, take up comfortable space:

- Sit with legs and arms uncrossed.
- Stand with wide, balanced stance.
- Avoid slouching or sinking into furniture.
- Extend arms to side tables/armrests.
- Relax muscles rather than constricting tightly.

Occupying space boosts comfort being seen and heard.

Slow down your pace

Rushed body language conveys nervousness. Force yourself to slow down:

- Walk at a steady, intentioned pace with head high.
- Pause between thoughts rather than quickly rambling.
- Make deliberate gesticulations.
- Take a deep breath before responding, not reacting quickly.

Controlled slowness projects poise and confidence.

Adjust body language style for context

Assertive body language differs between, say, a casual hangout versus asking for a promotion. Evaluate context:

- In formal settings, limit gestures and maintain serious demeanor.
- In conversations with superiors, keep movements conservative.
- When out with friends, relax and take up space comfortably.
- In public speaking, claim the stage with broad stances and expressions.

Fit body language to the situation while remaining authentic.

Listen with engaged posture

When others speak, look approachable and signal you're listening by:

- Turning your body to directly face them.
- Making interested facial expressions.
- Leaning in slightly rather than away.
- Avoiding distractions like phones.
- Providing affirming nods.

Mindful listening gives your assertiveness bidirectional strength.

The key is transforming assertive body language from something you have to consciously remember to adopt into an authenticexpression of your confidence and leadership presence. With regular practice, it becomes natural self-expression. You've got this!

Chapter 20: Reframing Negative Self-Talk

The inner critic is one of the biggest obstacles to developing assertiveness. Unpacking and reframing negative self-talk is essential work.

Let's explore common forms of counterproductive inner voices holding you back, and strategies to reframe them:

"It's Selfish/Greedy"

Pursuing your needs often triggers this inner attack. Counter it:

● Remind yourself self-care permits you to show up for others. You can't pour from an empty cup.

● Note you're modeling healthy boundaries others may lack.

● Remember that prioritizing your well-being does not detract from anyone else's worth. There's no shortage of compassion to go around.

You deserve to be fulfilled and content too. Don't let scarcity thinking shame you.

"I Don't Want to Be Difficult"

People-pleasing habits breed this hesitance to assert needs that may inconvenience or bother others. Retort with:

● Part of maturity is learning to have difficult conversations skillfully. You can handle it.

● You're teaching others how to treat you. Establish positive patterns now.

● Trust that reasonable people will respect you setting fair boundaries.

● Remember that stifling yourself fosters resentment on both sides.

You are worth the temporary difficulty. Don't confuse complicity for kindness.

"It's Not That Serious"

You likely minimize grievances, especially in family relationships. But small issues aggregate, so address them:

- The frequency of micro-aggressions adds up over time to impact your self-worth.
- Little issues you dismiss mount and eventually erupt angrily over seemingly small incidents.
- Speaking up teaches others your feelings and boundaries matter.
- Unchecked behavior continues without feedback.

Don't allow "death by a thousand cuts." Your needs deserve to be taken seriously.

"I Don't Want to Overreact"

You may have habits of subduing emotional reactions harshly. Temper this urge by:

- Remembering emotions convey valuable needs to be understood, not problems to extinguish.
- Developing nuance between reactive escalation and clear self-expression. The latter is healthy.
- Asking yourself what a proportionate outward response would be.
- Talking it through with trusted friends.

Suppressing emotions breeds pain. Don't numb yourself to avoid discomfort.

"Things Could Be Worse"

You likely guilt yourself out of assertiveness by noting things could always be worse. But this invalidates real issues. Acknowledge challenges you face without comparing. Your feelings are valid no matter how small issues may seem relative to others' hardships. Don't minimize your lived experience.

"I Should Be Better at This by Now"

Imposter syndrome makes you feel you should handle situations perfectly already. Remind yourself:

- Skills require consistent practice to develop. You're still learning.

- Everyone messes up social interactions sometimes. It's part of being human.
- Progress includes missteps. Criticize yourself constructively but also celebrate wins.
- Your value isn't defined by handling everything flawlessly.

Have compassion for the ups and downs of growing assertiveness skills. One step forward and two back is still progress.

"I Don't Deserve Better"

You may feel unworthy of caring treatment, especially if raised with conditional love. But remember:

- You deserve respect simply for being a human being. Your worth isn't earned through people-pleasing.
- Accepting poor treatment reinforces low self-esteem.
- Assertiveness builds your intrinsic view of your value over time.
- You teach others how you expect to be treated.

You are worthy of dignity, compassion, and fulfillment. Don't accept less.

Learning to reframe self-limiting narratives into empowering perspectives takes practice. But doing this inner work liberates you to stand up for yourself time and time again.

"I don't want to hurt their feelings"

It's natural to avoid saying anything that could upset others. But remember:

- Speaking tactfully avoids unnecessary harm.
- Some discomfort from the truth is needed for growth.
- Avoiding issues causes more hurt long-term through mounting resentment.
- Your feelings and boundaries matter too.

With care for yourself and them, important conversations become possible.

"It's just not my place"

There's a tendency to assume advocating for yourself is overstepping somehow. Counter this by:

● Reminding yourself that you have a right to respect and fair treatment like everyone else.

● Your viewpoints and needs are just as valid as others' are.

● Progress requires learning to speak up to address issues constructively.

● You aren't being arrogant, just authentic.

You belong at the table. Don't minimize your worth and voice.

"I'll seem unreasonable"

Speaking up assertively can feel like an extreme overreaction if you're used to staying silent. Adjust perspective:

● You aren't being unreasonable just by sharing your viewpoint respectfully.

● If others do react defensively, that's on them, not you.

● Unchecked behavior continues without feedback.

● There's no need to be aggressive. Thoughtful assertion creates change.

You are allowed to stand up for yourself. Others' potential discomfort shows that assertion is needed. Have courage.

"Things will never change"

Passivity often stems from fatalistic assumptions you're powerless. But reminding yourself:

● Your actions do impact others once you find your voice.

● By addressing issues assertively, you create potential for change.

● Your courage inspires courage in others observing you.

● Change may feel impossible until suddenly it isn't.

Pessimism justifies inaction. Have faith in your agency. You can do this!

"I'm too sensitive"

You may criticize yourself for taking things too personally when you get upset. But tell yourself:

- Emotions convey important messages - don't numb them.
- Your sensitivity allows you to empathize with others too.
- You're not being irrational just by having hurt feelings.
- Allowing yourself to feel builds emotional intelligence.

Reframe sensitivity as an asset, not a flaw.

"It's too awkward and uncomfortable"

Facing social discomfort keeps many stuck in passivity. But remind yourself:

- Tolerating short-term awkwardness leads to long-term fulfillment.
- The discomfort signifies an opportunity for growth.
- You'll build confidence each time you lean into uncertainty.
- You deserve to advocate for your wellbeing, even if difficult socially.

Discomfort is subjective - you control whether to shrink from it or face it.

"I'm incapable of being assertive"

Past failures or judgment from others may fuel this belief. But remember:

- Assertiveness is a skill you build, not an innate trait you lack.
- With practice and role models, new habits can be learned.
- Progress takes time, persistence and self-compassion.
- Every small step forward counts as growth to celebrate.

Don't accept limiting narratives others placed on you. Write your own story.

"It's pointless to bother"

If assertiveness has been punished or dismissed in your past, it's easy to see it as futile. But:

- Just because some reject feedback doesn't mean the effort was wasted.
- You may plant seeds of self-reflection that encourage change down the road.
- Speaking up demonstrates you are willing to be increasingly assertive over time if needed.

● You build personal integrity through courageous communication, regardless of the outcome.

Assert yourself because it aligns with your values, not just to control reactions.

Keep catching limiting thought patterns holding you back so you can progress to empowering inner dialogues that enable assertiveness. You've got this!

Chapter 21: Setting Healthy Boundaries

Setting clear boundaries and enforcing them consistently is essential for developing assertiveness.

Let's discuss how to establish healthy boundaries in various contexts along with strategies to reinforce them.

Identifying Reasonable Boundaries

Reflect on types of behaviors or treatment that you find unacceptably disrespectful such as:

- Demeaning or offensive jokes/comments
- Being yelled at or belittled
- Micromanagement undermining your capabilities
- Chronic lateness wasting your time
- Personal items/space being used without permission
- Having your emotional needs frequently ignored

You deserve to set standards for how you reasonably expect to be treated. Don't tolerate devaluation.

Communicating Boundaries Upfront

Don't wait until a boundary is crossed to express it. Gently set expectations proactively:

- Frame the need positively - what you want to see more of vs what you don't.
- Keep it simple rather than over-explaining.
- Make the language clear and specific to prevent misunderstandings.
- Highlight how it benefits the relationship.
- Offer to reciprocally honor their boundaries.

Setting expectations early creates understanding and prevents future issues.

Enforcing Boundaries Consistently

Occasional boundary crossings must be addressed quickly and directly to prevent escalation:

- Politely but firmly restate the violated boundary.
- Clarify exactly what you found unacceptable.
- Note you will need to end the interaction if it continues.
- Walk away if the behavior persists after a warning.
- Avoid engaging until the person demonstrates renewed respect.

Following through consistently trains people your boundaries cannot be ignored without consequence.

Practice Saying No

Many passive people struggle to simply say "No, I will not/cannot do that." But declining unreasonable requests and favors you resentfully accept is essential.

Ways to say no gracefully:

- "I'm not able to take that on, but thank you for thinking of me."
- "I don't have the bandwidth currently, but perhaps in the future."
- "I'm going to have to say no to that, but I appreciate you reaching out."
- "That won't work for me, but please let me know if I can help in any other way."

You aren't obligated to yes. Prioritize your needs and limits.

Set Time Boundaries

Limit how much time you give to draining activities or people. Note you have other commitments requiring your attention:

- "I'm happy to help for about 15 minutes but will have to get going after that."
- "I can call for a quick check-in but don't have time for a lengthy vent session today."
- "Let's limit happy hour to an hour since I have an early morning."
- Schedule activities after draining commitments to force you to move on.

You control your schedule. People-please less by capping how much you give.

Don't Justify or Defend

When setting boundaries, avoid over-explaining yourself or immediately caving if the person pushes back.

Simply restate your boundary clearly if challenged:

- "I'm not willing to take on additional responsibilities beyond the scope of my role."
- "I can't loan you any more money right now."
- "I'm not comfortable with you using my home without me here."

Short, direct statements leave little opening for manipulation or debate. You don't owe long defenses.

Remember - you teach others how you expect to be treated. Model setting and enforcing healthy boundaries, and relationships will flourish with mutual care and respect.

Identify boundary pushers

Note relationships where you find yourself repeatedly backing down on stated boundaries. These dynamics require repair:

- Discuss the pattern directly and restate your needs clearly.
- Commit to consistency - don't make exceptions that undermine the boundary.
- Stand firm on proportional consequences when tested.
- Evaluate if certain people are unwilling to respect your boundaries long-term.

You deserve relationships where your boundaries are honored.

Set financial boundaries

Money issues often strain relationships. To avoid this:

- Discuss financial values openly to ensure you're aligned.
- State what you will and won't share expenses wise upfront.
- Don't feel pressured into combining finances prematurely with partners. Move at your own pace.
- Loan money only if you're genuinely comfortable with the risk.
- Don't allow guilt around others' needs to push your boundaries.

Financial strains corrode intimacy. Handle money matters thoughtfully and assertively.

Redirect boundary crossers

When someone immediately pushes your boundary, redirect them:
- "I understand you want__, but I'm not willing to __."
- "While I appreciate the invitation, I'll have to decline."
- "I know you need support right now, but I'm at capacity. How else can I help?"

Politely reiterate your stance while offering alternative solutions.

Know you may lose some people

Accept that poorly matched or manipulative people may walk away when you start enforcing fair boundaries. While painful, this frees space for healthier relationships with others who respect your standards.

You deserve reciprocal consideration. Don't compromise reasonable boundaries in order to keep harmful people around.

Assertive communication paired with compassion allows you to set relationship standards that honor your needs while also showing genuine care. With practice, you can do this gracefully.

Set boundaries with authority figures

It can be intimidating to set boundaries with bosses, elders, or "important" people. But remembering:
- Your worth and rights don't diminish with lower professional status.
- Their authority in one domain does not extend to all domains.
- Challenge internalized pressure to obey at your own expense.
- You can stand firm respectfully.

Don't let position power differential coerce your boundaries.

Observe others' examples

Notice peers who balance self-care with caring for others. Model their boundaries around:

- Speaking up about workload capacity
- Leaving work at reasonable hours
- Not responding to emails after hours/on vacation
- Saying no to non-essential meetings and tasks

Let positive role models inspire your own assertiveness.

Set social media boundaries

Online connections require boundaries too:

- Limit time consuming reactive scrolling.
- Decline invitations to discuss polarizing issues.
- Unfollow accounts that frequently upset you.
- Keep personal details and information limited.

Don't let digital contacts drain you. Curate your spaces thoughtfully.

Remember progress takes time

Standing up for yourself often feels awkward and uncomfortable at first after a lifetime of passivity. Be patient with the process and celebrate each small win.

You deserve relationships that respect your consent and emotional health. With compassion and courage, you can do this.

Chapter 22: Becoming Assertive in Family Relationships

Family relationships often present the biggest challenges for setting boundaries and communicating assertively. Old roles, emotional triggers, and engrained dynamics embed deep.

However, bringing increased assertiveness into these complex relationships can profoundly change them for the better. Let's explore strategies tailored for family interactions.

With Siblings

Depending on birth order, siblings may still subconsciously try to boss each other around or assume familiar family roles. Disrupt this pattern by:

- Politely but firmly stating if a sibling tries delegating tasks or making plans for your time without your input. You are equals now.
- Noting your differing perspectives if they misrepresent your beliefs to outsiders to avoid conflict. Don't let them be your spokesman.
- Pushing back if they make jokes at your expense that touch on childhood wounds or sensitivities. You don't have to laugh along now.
- Thanking them for past support but reiterating that you make your own choices as an adult if they try directing your life decisions.

You can care deeply for one another while also reshaping dysfunctional patterns that carried over from childhood.

With Extended Family

Aunts, uncles, grandparents etc. may pry, offer outdated advice, or criticize your life choices at family events. Manage this by:

- Polite but brief answers if pressed about topics you want to avoid like dating life, weight, career etc. Change the subject.
- Offering neutral acknowledgment if they offer unsolicited opinions on your private life. Then move the conversation along.

- Pushing back gently if they make remarks that are racist, sexist, homophobic or otherwise intolerant now that you're an independent adult. Make your updated worldview known.
- Not becoming defensive if traditional older relatives question your modern career, family choices etc. Calmly reinforce it's your life to lead.

You can still show respect while also standing up for the person you've become.

During Holidays

Holidays with extended family in cramped spaces often exacerbate conflict and boundary issues. Cope by:
- Asking to review proposed holiday location/plans with input if family just informs you without checking availability.
- Getting a rental nearby but not directly with family so you have personal space to decompress after tense interactions.
- Volunteering to help with cooking, cleaning etc. to allow brief breaks from family time throughout the holidays.
- Booking your return ticket for early if tensions run high. It's better to politely leave than reach total meltdown.

You can maintain family bonds without completely sacrificing your emotional health. Set those assertive boundaries.

Redefining family relationships as an adult can feel intimidating, but clear communication and consistency over time transforms bondS for the better. You deserve healthy relationships with mutual care, respect and consideration. Keep advocating boldly but compassionately for the healthiest version of family.

With a spouse's family

In-law dynamics come loaded with expectations. Handle discomfort skillfully:
- Politely discuss traditions with your spouse you're unwilling to sacrifice.
- Offer to host or help cook to contribute joyfully on your own terms.
- Take occasional breaks during longer visits to decompress alone.

• Clarify when input is welcome versus when decisions are just being announced.

• Focus on finding common ground.

You can build healthy bonds without subsuming your identity.

Around addiction or abuse

Don't tolerate mistreatment just because it's family. Remove yourself from:

• Conversations turning hostile.

• Unsafe driving.

• Being berated or belittled.

• Physical intimidation.

• Pressure to enable addictive or destructive behaviors.

You are still capable of loving detachment. Protect yourself first.

With estranged family

If contacted by estranged family members, reflect first before responding:

• Why did you cut off contact originally? Have those conditions changed?

• Consult trusted friends to check your instincts against wisdom.

• Reply on your own time after careful consideration, not impulsive reaction.

• Start slow if reconnecting - don't overcommit.

• Create new patterns of positive relating before fully letting your guard down.

Cautious engagement preserves progress while still permitting change.

When setting new boundaries

Expect resistance when implementing new boundaries or redefining homecoming traditions:

• Compassionately but firmly reinforce this is what works for you now.

• Suggest slowly easing traditions into new patterns over time.

• Offer compromises to show you still wish to connect on their terms too sometimes.

- Remind them relationships grow through adaptation.
- With consistently loving enforcement, new norms develop.

Change takes time. Transition compassionately but resolutely.

You can develop assertive yet caring communication habits over time to transform even entrenched family dynamics for the healthier. Have hope!

Chapter 23: Developing Assertiveness in Intimate Relationships

Intimate relationships often reveal our deepest triggers and vulnerabilities, requiring courage and care to navigate assertively. Let's explore strategies for addressing tricky dynamics with partners.

Discussing Commitment Differences

Partners may desire different levels of commitment or have different timelines for milestones. Avoid unilateral decisions:

- Share your vision for the relationship's future openly even if it feels awkward. Full disclosure is key.
- If not aligned, discuss what needs and fears underlie these differences. Search for root common ground.
- Do not pressure, guilt-trip, or deliver ultimatums. Make requests gently.
- Compromise where possible, like a privately committed relationship before officially moving in.
- But know when to walk away if major life goals fundamentally conflict.

Honest conversations about needs, even if uncomfortable, prevent worse heartbreak down the road.

Facing Infidelity

Discovering a partner's infidelity is crushing. But avoid knee-jerk aggression when confronting:

- Take space to process intense emotions before discussing. Calm down first.
- Speak in person when ready. Do not have high-stakes conversations via text/email.
- Explain how the betrayal made you feel using "I" language. Do not attack their character.
- Allow them space to take accountability and explain what needs were unmet.

● Listen fully before deciding next steps. Consider counseling first before automatically separating.

There are no perfect victims or villains after affairs. Compassion on both sides enables working through wounds.

Coping with Mental Health Issues

Do not abandon struggling partners. Support them assertively:

● Research their condition to understand symptoms and treatments.

● Clarify how best to express care based on their personal needs.

● Set boundaries around your own limits and emotional health. You cannot be their therapist.

● Remind them consistently you see their value as a whole person, not just their illness.

● Evaluate with professionals when hospitalization, medication change or other intervention is needed.

With empathy, education and boundaries, you can sustain the relationship without absorbing their suffering.

Dividing Chores & Mental Load

Don't quietly martyr yourself doing the bulk of domestic tasks. Assert fairness:

● Make requests rather than resentful hints about needing help.

● Discuss each other's standards so mismatched expectations around tidiness don't breed contempt.

● Divide and rotate chores clearly. Adjust with changes like having kids.

● If scheduling is the issue, set reminders to share responsibility.

● Make sure you aren't shouldering the entire emotional burden of keeping track of social obligations, household needs etc.

Shifting domestic dynamics openly prevents buildup of one-sided resentment.

Discussing Major Career Moves

With partners on separate career paths, unilateral decisions impact everyone. Collaborate:

● Thoroughly research options together - location, salary, lifestyle changes etc.

● Weigh how choices align with joint priorities like starting a family, proximity to relatives etc.

● Determine where you're willing or unwilling to compromise.

● Agree on trial periods and checkpoints after deciding to reevaluate if needed.

● Make sure both partners get equal say - do not pressure or coerce big changes.

Ignoring a partner's needs breeds chronic resentment. But collaborative compromise enables managing transitions thoughtfully together.

Facing grief as a couple

Losing loved ones impacts relationships. Help each other through grief assertively:

● Allow each other space to grieve in your own way without judgement. People process loss differently.

● Set clear expectations around family responsibilities to avoid tensions.

● Verbalize increased needs for comfort and connection during the mourning period.

● Understand grieving impacts intimacy drives differently. Compromise sensitively.

● Check-in on each other's mental health and seek counseling if needed.

● Healing takes time. Have patience and lean on community support.

With empathy and teamwork, couples can support each other through grief's ebbs and flows.

Relational assertiveness ensures your intimate partner feels valued and understood, while also respecting your own emotional well-being. With courage and care, you can navigate conflict and growth together.

When a partner shuts down

Stonewalling kills intimacy. If they disengage from discussion, re-engage by:

- Giving them space to cool off before calmly readdressing the issue.
- Validating their emotions. "I know this conversation is upsetting. Can we work through this together when we've settled down?"
- Suggesting a code word you can say if needing to pause talks getting too heated.
- Focusing the goal on conflict resolution through compromise rather than attacking their withdrawal.

With patience, you can teach them healthy relating builds strength.

Facing codependency

Codependents lose sense of self in relationships. Regain independence through:

- Rediscovering activities and friends separate from your partner.
- Catching yourself when morphing preferences to match theirs.
- Saying no to requests out of obligation, not desire.
- Noticing when you silence your needs to avoid displeasing them. Speak up.
- Getting comfortable doing things independently that you always jointly participated in.
- Reminding yourself that the healthiest love has two strong, complete individuals choosing to be together, not needing each other to be whole.

You can regain self-sufficiency while still being a caring partner.

Acknowledging abusive dynamics

Don't ignore or minimize abusive patterns like:

- Demeaning, insulting language
- Isolating you from friends and family
- Explosive outbursts
- Physical intimidation
- Punishing emotionally when you assert boundaries

Seek help immediately. Your safety is priority one.

Learning to stand up for yourself around an intimate partner can be challenging, but also deeply rewarding. Handle conflict with care, choose your battles, and remain anchored in mutual goals and values. With courage, empathy and perseverance, even the most complex relationship dynamics can evolve to become more fulfilling and supportive.

Chapter 24: Becoming More Assertive in Meetings

Meetings provide frequent opportunities to practice assertiveness, from proposing ideas to navigating group dynamics. Stepping into greater leadership presence in meetings builds confidence.

Let's look at strategies to become more vocal and influential participant in meetings and workshops.

Come Prepared to Contribute

You can't confidently share ideas without preparation. Do your homework:

- Review the agenda and your own talking points.
- Research participants and conversation topics expected.
- Write down key questions and insights to share.
- Prepare any relevant data, stories, or examples to support your points.
- Practice articulating your perspective aloud to gain confidence.

Thorough preparation breeds the confidence to contribute meaningfully.

Volunteer Opinions Early

Your participation momentum builds by speaking up early. Find opportunities to share your perspective around welcoming points on the agenda like:

- The opening group check-in.
- When the facilitator asks easy icebreaker or get-to-know-you questions.
- During approval of past meeting minutes and agenda review when it's straightforward.

Starting with low-stakes comments builds momentum to assert yourself more over time.

Pose Thoughtful Questions

Asking intelligent clarifying questions has multiple benefits:

- It signals engaged, critical thinking.
- Draws out alternative perspectives.

- Allows you to proactively steer the conversation.
- Helps synthesize ideas into key takeaways.

Leverage judicious questioning to showcase your active listening and leadership potential.

Reference Others' Remarks

Citing points raised by colleagues makes your own remarks more persuasive while also demonstrating attentive listening:

- "Building on what John said earlier, I believe..."
- "You make an excellent point about __. Piggybacking off that..."
- "I agree with Sarah's recommendation. Additionally I suggest..."

Show you've paid attention to themes discussed and can synthesize them insightfully.

Find Your Entry Points

As an introvert, identify discrete entry points to share your perspective:

- When there's a direct opening like being invited to provide feedback.
- After someone else expresses a similar viewpoint that you can expand upon.
- By volunteering to summarize key takeaways or action items emerging.

Choose your moment thoughtfully when ready rather than interrupting blindly.

Redirect Back From Tangents

When meetings get off track, tactfully guide them back on course:

- "Those are all good points, but just to make sure we stay focused, the core issue we need to address is..."
- "You raise a fair concern. Perhaps we can discuss solutions offline so that we can get back to the central agenda item at hand?"
- "I want to be cognizant of folks' time. Could we table the periphery concerns for now and prioritize the planned discussion points?"

Politely get things back on track like an assertive coordinator.

Bridge Disagreements Diplomatically

When colleagues clash, serve as a mediator:

- Restate the key common ground or shared goals of both parties to unite them.
- Ask clarifying questions to better understand each perspective. Avoid taking sides.
- Offer win-win compromises that allow each side to feel partly satisfied.
- Suggest tabling heated conflicts to revisit when cooler heads may prevail.

Rising above the fray distinguishes your leadership potential.

Practicing assertive habits in low-stakes meetings builds confidence to eventually guide high-stakes discussions. Be prepared, fully present, and steadfastly professional. With consistency, you will grow into a highly valued contributor.

Speak up about interruptions

If you get frequently interrupted or spoken over, politely intervene:

- "Excuse me, I wasn't quite finished making my point."
- "I'm sorry, I just want to complete my thought before we move on."
- "Let's please be mindful not to cut each other off so everyone can be heard."

You deserve space to fully express your perspective. Don't let yourself be silenced.

Manage dominating colleagues

If certain colleagues dominate airtime, politely regulate it:

- "In the interest of time, let's go around and hear from some folks we haven't yet."
- "Thank you for your thoughts. Moving forward, let's limit shares to two minutes each."
- Direct questions specifically to quieter members.

Make space for balanced contribution from all attendees.

Set expectations for off-topic tangents

If meetings frequently veer off track, set expectations:
- Request that side topics be tabled for after the meeting.
- Note when there are only 5-10 minutes remaining to complete agenda items.
- At the start, ask attendees to hold side conversations for breaks.
- Enforce timed agendas. When time is up, move to the next item.

Refocusing wandering meetings prevents unproductivity and frustration.

Push back on unrealistic expectations

If unreasonable commitments are pushed upon you, stand your ground:
- "I'm concerned about committing to that without discussing it more."
- "My current workload won't allow me to reasonably take that on."
- "I'd like work through potential roadblocks before agreeing to a deadline."

You have every right to protect your time and set realistic expectations. Just communicate sensitively.

Offer constructive feedback to leaders

Rather than staying silent about issues with those running the meetings:
- Politely share suggestions for improvement privately 1:1 after the meeting.
- Provide balanced feedback - point out what worked well in addition to issues.
- Use "I" statements like "I felt confused when..." rather than accusations.
- Offer win-win solutions rather than just criticizing.
- Thank them sincerely for being receptive if they handle your feedback maturely.

Speaking up constructively prevents long-term frustrations.

Don't stay silent when you disagree

Voice thoughtful disagreement assertively by:

- Expressing empathy first. "I understand your perspective, and appreciate the thought you've put into this."
- Briefly re-stating key points you agree with before noting disagreement.
- Using softening language like, "In my experience though, I've found..."
- Making suggestions rather than just rejecting ideas.
- Being open-minded. Allow your opinion to be influenced too.

Non-confrontational assertion of difference expands thinking.

Call out unprofessional behavior

If colleagues behave disrespectfully:

- Later, calmly but directly point out how the behavior affected you and the environment negatively.
- Assume good intent initially. Perhaps they were unaware of how they came across.
- Suggest solutions like keeping comments focused on content not attacking character.
- Notify HR if harassment persists after direct requests to cease.

You deserve respect. Don't enable unprofessional conduct through silence.

Practicing assertive communication consistently, whether in small check-in's or critical company presentations, builds influence and leadership capabilities over time. Keep at it!

Chapter 25: Use "I" Statements

One of the most important communication skills for being assertive is using "I" statements. "I" statements are a way of expressing your thoughts, feelings, and needs in a clear, respectful manner that avoids blaming others. Mastering "I" statements is essential for maintaining positive relationships while advocating for yourself.

What Are "I" Statements?

An "I" statement focuses the sentence on yourself and your experience using the pronoun "I", rather than using "you" which can sound accusatory. For example:
- "I feel frustrated when I am interrupted"
- "I would prefer if you gave me more notice before changing plans"

Versus:
- "You're frustrating me when you interrupt me"
- "You need to give me more notice when you change plans"

While the second phrasing isn't outright rude, it can easily provoke defensiveness in the other person. "I" statements avoid that confrontational tone.

Guidelines for "I" Statements

Effective "I" statements follow three simple guidelines:

Start with "I"

Put the focus on yourself and your own perspective. Avoid starting with "you" which can sound blaming even if that's not your intention.

Follow with a feeling or thought

Describe how you feel using clear feeling words like frustrated, upset, disappointed, etc. Or, describe your honest thoughts about the situation.

End with a need or request

Conclude by expressing what you need or requesting a specific change in behavior. This gives the other person clear direction.

Examples

Here are some examples of using "I" statements in both personal and professional situations:

- "I feel overwhelmed when you don't help with the housework. I would appreciate if you could take care of the dishes tonight." Here a spouse uses an "I" statement to make a request about sharing chores.

- "I was really hurt when you cancelled our plans last minute. In the future, I need at least 24 hours notice before changing plans." A friend uses an "I" statement to set a boundary after their plans were changed.

- "I feel frustrated when you interrupt me during meetings. I would like a chance to finish my thoughts before you give your input." An employee uses an "I" statement to set a boundary with an interrupting coworker.

- "I feel nervous presenting in front of the team. It would help build my confidence if I could start with a few smaller presentations first." An "I" statement used to make a request of a manager.

- "I feel upset that my assignment was given to Jill without discussing it with me first. In the future, I would appreciate being consulted before reassigning my projects." An "I" statement expressing feelings about a project being reassigned without notice.

Let's break down each example:

Housework Request

This "I" statement has three clear parts:

I feel overwhelmed when you don't help with the housework. (expresses feelings)

I would appreciate if you could take care of the dishes tonight. (makes a specific request)

By saying "I feel overwhelmed" the spouse avoids an accusatory "you never help me" and instead focuses on how the situation impacts them. Making a polite request gives their partner clear direction for a desired behavior change.

Changing Plans

This "I" statement follows the same format:

I was really hurt when you cancelled our plans last minute. (expresses thoughts and feelings)

In the future, I need at least 24 hours notice before changing plans. (states a clear need)

The person expresses that cancelling plans made them feel hurt without blaming their friend as insensitive. They also establish a clear boundary needed from this person.

Interrupting Coworker

In this workplace example, the "I" statement sounds like this:

I feel frustrated when you interrupt me during meetings. (shares feelings)

I would like a chance to finish my thoughts before you give your input. (makes a request)

The employee sticks to their own perspective that the interrupting makes them feel frustrated. They politely request the desired behavior change.

Requesting Smaller Presentations

Here is the "I" statement structure:

I feel nervous presenting in front of the team. (expresses feelings)

It would help build my confidence if I could start with a few smaller presentations first. (makes a request)

This person is honest about their anxiety and how the requested change would help them. There's no tone of accusation or forcing their manager to change.

Reassigned Project

Finally, this "I" statement:

I feel upset that my assignment was given to Jill without discussing it with me first. (shares feelings)

In the future, I would appreciate being consulted before reassigning my projects. (requests desired behavior)

The employee honestly expresses upset feelings about their project being reassigned. They focus on wanting to be consulted first, rather than attacking their manager's judgement.

Why Use "I" Statements?

Using "I" statements to express your needs and boundaries in a thoughtful, polite manner leads to much better outcomes than avoiding the conversation or using an aggressive, blaming tone.

Some specific benefits of "I" statements for assertive communication:

● Reduces defensiveness. Using "I" lowers people's instinct to become defensive and makes them more receptive to your message.

● Avoids escalation. "I" statements encourage a calmer, more constructive conversation without angry accusations.

● Focuses the issue. Using "I" keeps the discussion focused on finding a resolution that works for both people.

● Clarifies needs. "I" statements let people clearly understand what you need from them.

● Allows you to monitor yourself. Using "I" ensures you take responsibility for your own emotions and don't project feelings onto others.

● Models vulnerability. Sharing your feelings and thoughts honestly via "I" statements builds intimacy through mutual vulnerability.

● Keeps things simple. "I" statements avoid complex analyses of the other person's motivations and keep the message straightforward.

Put simply, "I" statements help you assert your needs in a way people are far more likely to respond to positively. They lay the groundwork for compromise, not conflict.

Common Problems and Improvements

It takes practice to master speaking in "I" statements. Here are some common issues and how to improve:

Problem: You Lapse Into "You" Statements

Old habits creep in, and you start sentences with "you" instead of "I", sounding accusatory.

Improvement: Catch yourself when using "you" and rephrase the sentence in your head starting with "I". It takes awareness but this mental rephrasing will become second nature over time.

Problem: You're Too Vague

Instead of clear feeling words, you use vague statements like "I feel bad" or "I feel weird."

Improvement: Get comfortable using specific feeling words. Make a list of words for different emotions to broaden your emotional vocabulary.

Problem: You Criticize Instead of Expressing Feelings

Rather than saying "I feel hurt", you state criticism like "I feel like you don't value me."

Improvement: Separate your feelings from judgments about the other person's motivations. Stick to owning your feelings and asking for what you need.

Problem: You Make Impersonal Requests

You say "I want this task completed" instead of connecting the request to your personal needs.

Improvement: Elaborate on why you need what you're requesting. For example, "I'm feeling overwhelmed and need help with this task." Don't just make demands.

Problem: You Have Trouble Making Direct Requests

You hint at what you want instead of asking directly and clearly.

Improvement: Practice making requests until you can comfortably say what you need. Remember a clear request leaves less room for confusion.

"I" Statements for Professional Growth

While we've covered personal examples, using "I" statements effectively is just as important in workplace environments for advocating your needs.

Whether asking for a promotion, a raise, more responsibility, or different working conditions, "I" statements help you achieve professional growth diplomatically.

Some examples of using "I" statements at work:

- "I've really enjoyed taking the lead on the last few marketing campaigns. I feel ready to manage the marketing department and would love to be considered for the manager position."
- "I feel I've exceeded my sales targets this past year and brought in high-value clients. I believe my performance warrants a 10% raise in my salary."
- "I feel capable of taking on more responsibility directing corporate events. I'd appreciate the opportunity to coordinate the next client retreat."
- "I feel overwhelmed trying to balance all my projects right now. I need to offload some work to another team member to manage my stress levels."

No matter your profession or work environment, "I" statements help you self-advocate and create win-win solutions. Managers are far more receptive to employee needs framed with "I" instead of demands, complaints or threats.

Don't Forget Empathy

While "I" statements focus on expressing your own perspective, it's still important to balance that with empathy for the other person. Make sure to truly listen and acknowledge their viewpoint too.

You can pair an "I" statement with empathy like:

- *"I felt concerned when I had to cover for you last week. I know you've been dealing with a lot at home right now. In the future, I would appreciate more notice so I can plan my workload accordingly."*

This shows you care about their situation while still making a request for the future. Blending empathy into an "I" statement makes it even more effective.

Summary

Learning to communicate assertively with "I" statements instead of passive or aggressive speech takes dedication, self-awareness, and practice. But it is one of the most rewarding communication skills you can develop for emotional intelligence and advocating for your needs while protecting relationships.

Some key points to remember:
- Use "I feel" to express thoughts and emotions
- Follow up with clear needs and requests
- Avoid blaming "you" language
- Focus on understanding the other perspective too
- It takes practice so be patient with yourself!

Start paying attention to when you can turn statements with "you" or impersonal demands into "I" statements. With time, you'll find these become natural for you.

The better you become at asserting your needs via "I" statements, the more easily you'll move toward healthier, happier relationships and work environments.

Chapter 26: Pick Battles Wisely

When learning to be more assertive, it's important to choose your battles. Not every unreasonable demand or frustrating situation calls for an assertive response. You have to consider when it's worth speaking up versus letting something go.

Picking battles wisely preserves your emotional energy for the issues that truly matter. You'll face less resentment and approach challenging conversations calmly.

Here are some strategies to help determine when assertiveness is most appropriate and when it's better to save your energy.

Is This a Repeated Pattern?

Think through whether this is an isolated incident or part of a repeating pattern of behavior. If it's a rare occurrence, you may opt to let it go. But if it's becoming a habit that disrespects your boundaries, it's time to address it assertively.

For example, your partner being late to one date night is annoying but not a pattern. Them being late repeatedly shows disrespect deserving an assertive conversation.

Or a coworker making one insensitive remark can be ignored as an innocent mistake. But repeated remarks create a hostile environment needing assertive action.

Pay attention to patterns. Don't overreact to single incidents, but don't let people establish disrespectful habits either.

Am I Overly Emotional Right Now?

Before reacting assertively, examine your current emotional state. Are you very angry, hurt or otherwise emotional about the situation? If so, your emotions may be clouding your judgment.

You risk escalating the encounter if you're in a reactive state. The other person also won't receive your message well if you appear overly emotional.

If you feel very upset, take time to cool down first. Revisit the issue later objectively. A level head allows you to be calm but firm.

Is This Truly Important?

Consider your priorities and decide whether the issue is worth taking a stand on. How much does it truly matter to you? Is it interfering with your core values and needs?

For minor annoyances, it's often best to let things go and save your energy. But if it's obstructing things you care deeply about, then assertiveness is warranted.

Knowing your must-haves helps judge whether a given situation is important enough to address assertively. Don't sweat the small stuff but stand firm on your deal-breakers.

Does It Directly Impact Me?

Before reacting, ask if the offending behavior or situation directly impacts you or harms your own interests. If not, considering letting it go. But if it does affect you, assertion is often appropriate.

For example, a coworker arriving late doesn't directly impact you. But them missing your shared project deadline does, warranting assertion.

Likewise, a friend's personal choice that doesn't harm you can be accepted. But them breaking plans with you affects you directly and merits discussion.

Consider where the situation falls on the spectrum of impacting you directly or tangentially when deciding to assert yourself or not.

Am I Being Too Rigid?

Examine whether your own inflexibility or stubbornness may be contributing to the problem. Are you unwilling to give any ground or compromise? Does it have to be your way or no way at all?

If you're failing to empathize with the other perspective or refusing to meet halfway, becoming more flexible may resolve the issue. Pick battles where you have clearly communicated your needs but they remain unmet.

Will Speaking Up Lead to Resolution?

Consider the likelihood that asserting yourself will lead to a productive resolution versus escalating conflict further. Will the person truly hear you and collaborate on a solution?

If discussion seems fruitless or even dangerous, you may have to accept suboptimal situations for now. But if a pathway exists for mutual understanding, then assertion is worthwhile.

Can I Speak Respectfully?

Ask yourself if you can have the conversation calmly and respectfully. Or will you lapse into hurtful remarks and anger?

Productive assertion requires a level head. If emotions are running too high for a civil discussion, wait until you can speak rationally and empathetically.

Am I Avoiding Out of Fear?

Sometimes we avoid asserting ourselves due to fear of confrontation, rejection, or looking selfish. Examine if a fear response rather than logic is guiding your choice to accept the status quo.

Don't let anxiety talk you out of having difficult but necessary conversations. Lean into growth by asserting yourself despite the discomfort.

Will My Timing Make It Worse?

Consider whether now is the right time and place to have the talk or if waiting for a better moment will improve your odds of a good outcome.

For example, addressing an issue at work privately may be better than criticizing someone publicly in a meeting. And discussing a marital issue when calm rather than in the heat of an argument can help.

Think strategically about setting yourself up for success with your timing and situation. But don't indefinitely delay vital conversations.

Am I Being Overly Accommodating?

Examine whether a pattern of being overly passive, conflict avoiding, and eager to please is leading you to accept situations you should be asserting boundaries on.

A tendency to accommodate at your own expense makes it hard to know when to push back. Building your overall assertiveness helps identify the right battles.

Is This a Deal Breaker for Me?

Finally, consider whether the issue warrants ending a relationship over if unresolved. But be very cautious about threatening the nuclear option without attempts to communicate, understand, and compromise.

Reserve deal breaker stances only for issues core to your ethics and happiness. But be open to working through problems before jumping to relationship termination.

Choosing Battles at Work

Navigating when to push back on issues versus letting things go is an essential workplace skill too. Choose your battles to avoid unnecessary friction while advocating for your needs.

Some questions to help determine whether to assert yourself at work:

• Does this directly impair my ability to meet expectations and perform well?

• Is the issue hindering my work, well-being or professional growth?

• Have I already attempted reasonable compromises before escalating this?

• Will speaking up improve the situation or make it worse?

• Can I have a constructive dialogue about this with my supervisor?

• Is my concern in alignment with company policy and culture?

• Am I picking this battle for my own ego versus the greater good?

• Are my expectations realistic and being communicated respectfully?

• Is this the right time and place to raise this concern?

Analyze whether asserting yourself is in service of your own and the organization's best interests. Don't sweat small annoyances, but speak up assertively when you or the work are being materially harmed.

Handling Repeat Offenders

When the same person repeatedly behaves disrespectfully, crosses your stated boundaries, or ignores your requests, stronger assertion is needed.

You may need to enforce increasing consequences. For example:

● Clearly communicate the problem behavior and your needs (first assertively, then more firmly if needed).

● Limit your exposure to the person if behavior doesn't improve.

● Loop in a supervisor or HR if attempts to resolve directly fail.

● Remove the person from your life as a last resort if the relationship becomes toxic.

Don't endlessly tolerate bad patterns. But pursue resolution through communication before cutting someone off completely.

Choosing Your Battles Wisely

Here are some final tips for learning to choose your battles judiciously:

Pick priorities. Decide your non-negotiable must-haves versus lower-priority preferences. Stay firm on the must-haves.

Accept occasional frustration. Tolerating mild annoyance sometimes is part of healthy relationships and workplaces. Don't react to every irritation.

Compromise when possible. Look for reasonable compromises before asserting yourself aggressively on an issue.

Wait for clarity. Sleep on a frustration before deciding if it's battle worthy. Time brings objectivity.

Trust your instincts. If your gut says a situation necessitates assertiveness, it likely does.

Start small. Build confidence addressing lower-stakes issues assertively before tackling really challenging ones.

Enforce boundaries. Repeatedly violated boundaries merit increased assertion. Don't let people trample your limits.

Choose dignity over drama. Resist the urge to "win" every disagreement. Focus on mutual understanding.

Know when to fold. Some circumstances warrant letting go instead of butting heads. Be able to walk away.

Keep perspective. Ask if this will matter in a year. Petty squabbles usually won't.

Learning when to stand up for yourself while also practicing wisdom in letting some things slide takes maturity. But choosing your battles carefully reduces stress while still upholding your boundaries. Set your intentions on win-win solutions, not escalating drama.

Summary

Deciding when being assertive is appropriate versus accepting imperfect situations is situational. But asking yourself key questions about patterns, priorities, timing, and conflict avoidance can guide you.

Pick battles where core values and direct well-being are at stake. Let minor slights go while maintaining boundaries on repeated issues. Mastering when to speak up and when to conserve energy serves all your relationships.

Chapter 27: Assert Your Needs in Relationships

Romantic relationships offer immense rewards but also require navigating each partner's differences and needs. Assertiveness helps you express your needs in a relationship while respecting your partner's perspective too.

While challenging, speaking up about issues is preferable to unspoken resentment breeding passive-aggressiveness or contempt. Mastering assertion fosters healthier, more satisfying bonds.

Here we'll explore strategies for asserting yourself diplomatically in romantic relationships.

Ensure a Foundation of Trust

Assertion has the best chance of success within stable relationships where trust and goodwill are already established. Don't wait until a crisis to start communicating assertively.

Early on, partners should:

● Bond by sharing experiences, interests, values, hopes and fears.

● Establish shared relationship priorities like commitment, growth, passion.

● Clarify fundamental compatibility on major issues like finances, future goals, intimacy needs.

● Build intimacy through affection, mutual support during hard times, enjoying activities together.

● Demonstrate dependability by consistently following through on promises and obligations.

● Nurture intimacy through great sex, laughing together, sharing feelings and dreams.

This foundation cements you as a team, giving the relationship strength to weather periods of conflict.

Have Discussions Versus Arguments

Don't assert controversial needs in the heat of high emotion or it will escalate into a destructive argument.

Instead, wait until you're both calm. Then:

● Set the tone that this is a thoughtful discussion, not a battle or attack.

● Affirm your love and commitment first so they don't feel threatened.

● Take turns to ensure you both fully express your perspective and feel heard.

● Don't interrupt or get defensive as the other shares. Listen sincerely.

● After explaining your viewpoint, ask curious clarifying questions to deepen understanding versus rebutting immediately.

● Find areas of agreement first before problem solving disagreements.

● Thank your partner for explaining their experience. Appreciate their openness.

● If things escalate, take a break to cool off and regain composure before reengaging.

Staying measured rather than reactive makes resolution possible. You're partners, not adversaries.

Pick a Suitable Time

Choose an optimal time to have challenging discussions where you're both calm and focused. Not when you're already arguing, exhausted, distracted, or pressed for time.

Schedule an uninterrupted period devoted to the talk rather than springing it on your partner out of the blue. Give forewarning of the topic so they aren't blindsided but don't obsess over it.

During the discussion, stick to one major issue rather than unloading every grievance. Don't run through your whole "list". Pick one meaningful topic and give it the focus it deserves.

Use "I" Statements

As explained in Chapter 25, asserting yourself via "I statements" is more effective than "you" accusations. Using "I" statements like:

- "I feel concerned when you cancel our dates last minute."
- "I need more quality time together to feel connected."

Reduces defensiveness and helps the other person understand your internal experience.

Avoid blaming statements like:

- "You're so inconsiderate when you cancel plans."
- "You never make me feel like a priority."

This provokes a fight-or-flight reaction, not mutual understanding.

Discuss One Issue at a Time

Don't overload your partner by tackling every grievance at once. Choose only the most pressing issue to focus on.

Trying to cover too many topics at once is overwhelming. It prevents the depth of understanding needed to find solutions.

Once you resolve one topic, schedule another discussion for the next priority area later. Breaking things into smaller pieces avoids feeling overwhelmed.

Listen Actively

While explaining your perspective, also make an effort to truly hear and understand where your partner is coming from.

Active listening requires:

- Giving them your full attention without multi-tasking. Make eye contact.
- Allowing them to fully express themselves without interrupting.
- Clarifying before rebutting: "So you're saying you feel I don't appreciate your efforts around the house?"
- Affirming their viewpoint: "I appreciate you explaining where you're coming from. I hadn't seen it that way."
- Summarizing their key points to confirm understanding.
- Asking thoughtful follow up questions, not just waiting for your turn to refute.
- Avoiding dismissive/invalidating language: "You shouldn't feel that way."

Make your partner feel genuinely listened to, not just heard. The deepest solutions flow from mutual understanding.

Find the Validity in Each Other's Perspectives

Rather than approaching the conversation combatively, look for validity in each other's stances.

You both likely have fair points mixed in with blind spots or exaggerations. Seek the truth in each view.

- They're not 100% right or wrong. Neither are you.
- Look for their good intentions behind frustrations. Give the benefit of the doubt.
- Recognize when your own perceptions may be incomplete or biased. We all have blind spots.
- Explore: How might each of you be right in different ways? What's fair and valid to me, you and us?
- Don't just tolerate their stance - find wisdom you can actually appreciate in it. And help them do the same for your view.

This prevents a partisan stalemate by illuminating solutions.

Validate Each Other's Feelings

Emotions are neither right or wrong - they simply exist as truth for each person.

Rather than fighting over whose feelings are more justified, start by validating each other's emotions:

- If your partner shares feeling unappreciated, don't argue they shouldn't feel that way. Recognize this is their sincere experience: "I understand you've been feeling really unappreciated and I want to understand more about why."
- Don't correct or debate feelings. The goal is understanding: "Help me understand why you felt belittled when I brought up that issue. I want to get where you're coming from better."
- Share your feelings using "I", not "you". model vulnerability: "I felt really rejected which is why I withdrew."

No matter how irrational they may seem to each other initially, your feelings make sense from your vantage points. Start there, then move to solutions.

Compromise and Problem Solve

Once you both fully understand each other's experiences, collaborate on win-win compromises or creative solutions.

- Brainstorm mutually satisfactory options, not just concessions to one side.
- Identify each person's core needs and work to meet them.
- Propose compromises and refine until a balance is reached.
- Discuss practical ways to prevent this issue going forward. How can each of you help?
- Schedule check-ins on progress. Adjust agreements if needed.
- Appreciate small gains to build momentum. Don't wait for perfection.

Focus on win-win resolutions, not winning the argument.

Don't Seek Total Agreement

Expecting your partner to fully agree with your position is unrealistic and unnecessary. The goal is mutual understanding and a solution that honors each viewpoint appropriately - not total submission.

You'll never see eye-to-eye on everything. Close relationships require compromise between two complex individuals with differences.

Value reaching an empathetic, "good enough" agreement you both feel decent about. Perfection is unattainable.

When to Compromise Versus Stand Firm

As discussed in Chapter 8, compromise doesn't always mean meeting in the middle. Sometimes it means taking turns getting your way.

On minor issues, taking turns or meeting halfway often works. But core values and dealbreakers shouldn't be compromised.

If standing up for a non-negotiable need, do so with empathy but firmness. Compromising on essential values damages your sense of self over time.

However, re-examine demands framed as "dealbreakers" that actually aren't. Don't confuse wants with needs. Clarify priorities.

Manage Expectations

Make sure you're expecting realistic changes, not perfection. People won't transform overnight. Manage expectations.

Agree on small incremental progress and metrics, not vague ultimatums.

For example, if asking your partner to get in shape:

Unrealistic expectation: "You need to become super fit."

Realistic expectation: "I'd appreciate if you went to the gym with me twice a week as a start."

Then build on small successes over time.

Appreciate Effort

When your partner makes a genuine effort to meet your needs better, notice and appreciate their initiative.

Don't take it for granted or move the goalposts requiring even more before you'll express approval. Recognize incremental progress.

Sincerely appreciating effort, even if the outcome isn't perfect yet, motivates sustained growth.

Own Your Part

While discussing your needs, also reflect on ways you may be contributing to the problem. Be willing to self-reflect and apologize.

- Could you have communicated in a more constructive way earlier?
- Do you need to be more tolerant at times?
- Have you made unfair assumptions?
- Are you asking them to address an insecurity of yours that's not their responsibility?
- Are you showing appreciation for their efforts?

Taking some ownership diffuses conflict and builds reciprocity. You're in it together.

Don't Tolerate Repeated Boundary Violations

Though aim for compromise, don't accept partners repeatedly violating your clear boundaries after you've communicated their importance.

Enforce consequences like:

● Requiring counseling if the issue stems from underlying relationship dynamics you can't solve independently. Get help.

● Taking a relationship break if your partner seems unwilling to understand your needs despite repeated attempts.

● Ultimately ending relationships with unresponsive partners who won't respect healthy boundaries.

Though always use these measures as a last resort.

Support Each Other's Growth

Partners should nurture each other's growth in being the best version of themselves. Not demanding change for its own sake or controlling how the other "should" be.

When asking your partner to improve in some way:

● Frame requests in terms of positive growth versus negatives to be fixed.

● Explain how the change will help them flourish as a person. Show you're on their side.

● Offer your active support in creating new habits. Do it together.

● Focus on strengths whilealso addressing areas for growth. We all have both.

Make your relationship an encouraging environment for mutual growth.

Maintain Intimacy

Don't let challenges put emotional distance between you. During conflicts, find ways to stay intimately connected:

● Shared activities you both enjoy

- Physical affection - hugs, hand holding, massages (no coerced intimacy)
- Reassuring each other your bond remains secure
- Appreciating what you love about your partner
- Humor and laughter to stay playful
- Sexting/flirting if appropriate
- A nice gesture like bringing home flowers or their favorite treat

This sustains your friendship until you reestablish harmony.

Seek Outside Perspective When Needed

If you repeatedly clash over an issue without progress, seeking outside input may help reveal blind spots.

Ask a neutral party like a therapist or respected couple you both trust for perspective.

An outside view sheds new light on dysfunctional patterns. But also take critiques with discernment - advice that resonates with you both is most valuable.

Summary

Navigating conflict successfully while asserting your needs requires mutual understanding and a spirit of growth, not winning arguments. Stay grounded in your friendship.

With empathy, vulnerability and consistent effort, assertion strengthens the relationship by keeping communication courageously open. Prioritize listening while standing firm on core values.

Though challenging, embracing assertion and compromise builds intimacy far more than avoiding difficult dialogues. You deepen bonds by expanding understanding of each other's inner worlds.

Chapter 28: Handle Aggressive Responses

When asserting yourself, some people may react aggressively and escalate the situation rather than respond calmly. Staying centered in the face of belligerence requires preparation and emotional control.

With practice, you can defend your boundaries while also avoiding unhealthy aggression of your own. Here are techniques for dealing with aggressive reactions.

Don't Match Aggression

Most importantly, resist the urge to meet aggression with your own aggressive responses. This only escalates the conflict which seldom persuades people to understand your viewpoint.

When others get heated and confrontational, double down on staying calm, rational and mature. Take the high road.

Channel any anger into an inner resolve to stand by your principles, not lashing out. Anger might be justified but rarely constructive.

Re-State Your Boundaries

If someone becomes hostile when you assert yourself, simply re-state your stance in a clear, controlled manner without getting reactive:

- "I understand you're getting upset, but this is my decision and I need you to respect it."
- "Getting aggressive with me won't change my mind. Let's please discuss this respectfully."
- "Shouting at me is not okay. I'm willing to talk about this when we can have a calm conversation."

Then, if they remain confrontational, give them space to cool off before attempting more dialogue. Disengage rather than sinking to their level.

Empathize Without Caving

In response to aggression, offer measured empathy about why they might feel that way, but reaffirm your right to your position:

- "I know you really want me to change my mind, and feeling disappointed makes sense. But I'm not willing to compromise here."
- "I get that not getting your way is frustrating. At the same time, attacking me won't make me back down."

Empathy helps diffuse anger while standing firm. Don't Give in simply to be agreeable.

Broken Record Technique

Some people try to wear you down, hoping you'll cave if they just keep pressure up.

Use the "broken record technique" - calmly repeating your statement word-for-word without being baited into aggression:

Them: "You're so selfish for refusing to loan me money again!"

You: "I understand you're upset, but I'm not willing to discuss this further right now."

Them: "Stop being so smug! I don't care what you say, I need that money!"

You: "I understand you're upset, but I'm not willing to discuss this further right now."

Them: "Ugh, forget it, you were always a terrible friend."

You: "I understand you're upset, but I'm not willing to discuss this further right now."

Staying unflappable in repeating your stance frustrates their attempts to manipulate you into compliance through intimidation.

Ask Them to Leave

If someone is being verbally abusive or won't calm down, ask them to leave the situation:

- "You seem very upset right now. Let's continue this conversation later once we can treat each other respectfully."

- "I'm going to leave if we can't discuss this calmly. I'll be ready to talk when heads are cooler."
- "This isn't productive. I'm going to hang up/walk away now. We can try again when we're both in a better space."

Don't tolerate mistreatment. But explain you're willing to reengage under healthier conditions. Then enforce that boundary.

Set Next-Step Consequences

Make the consequences clear if their aggression persists when attempting to discuss things again later:

"If you continue being hostile when we revisit this, I will have to take steps like:

- Leaving the situation immediately.
- Delaying further discussion for [time period] until we can converse respectfully.
- Involving [appropriate authority] if we can't find resolution on our own.
- Ending this relationship if treating each other with respect becomes impossible."

Calmly informing them of the escalating responses their aggression will elicit gives fair warning. Follow through consistently.

Document Serious Issues

If someone has recurring angry, threatening reactions that make you feel unsafe, document these incidents.

Write down dates, specific statements, witnesses present, and your requests to stop the behavior.

Documentation creates a record in case you ever need evidence to get law enforcement or authorities involved to restrict their contact with you.

Hopefully things never escalate to that level, but have documentation as a precaution if the situation becomes volatile enough.

Don't Take Anger Personally

Remember aggressive reactions reflect the other person's inner issues - not your worthiness.

Their anger often comes from feeling insecure, helpless or out of control when you challenge their viewpoint or power over you. Deep down, it's their problem, but you become their target.

View aggression as flowing from their psychological struggles, not anything you've done to deserve it. Maintain your self-confidence.

Use Strategic Body Language

Consciously project grounded, confident body language in response to aggression:

Eye contact: Look directly at the person (unless not recommended for your safety). Don't avert your gaze, which conveys discomfort or avoidance.

Posture: Stand or sit upright rather than slouching. Keep your chin level. Avoid crossed arms or legs, which project defensiveness. Take up space.

Hands: Keep hand movements minimal and purposeful versus fidgeting. Hands at your sides or on a table convey stability.

Facial expression: Maintain a calm, confident expression rather than reflecting their anger. Keep your mouth relaxed, not tight.

Voice: Speak slowly, firmly and smoothly. Don't raise your volume or pace. Warm confidence, not strained intensity, should come through.

Projecting unflappable assurance retains your position of strength.

Practice Staying Grounded

When you find yourself getting angry or flustered by confrontation, use quick techniques to regain composure:

Deep belly breathing - Slow inhales/exhales

"Grounding" exercise - Look around and name objects you see to redirect brain from emotion to logic.

Positive self-talk - Silently repeat affirmations like "I'm capable and in control."

Buy time - Take a bathroom break or pause to "gather your thoughts".

Inner visualization - Picture resolving scenario successfully. See your confidence.

With preparation, you can override combative reactions and remain focused.

Set Boundaries Around Future Contact

In ongoing relationships, set temporary boundaries until the person can treat you respectfully:

- No contact for a set period of time to process what occurred.
- Restricting conversations to email if talks escalate quickly. Removes real-time pressure.
- Public interactions only until trust/comfort rebuild. Harder to be aggressive with an audience.
- No discussion of hot button topics likely to spark defensiveness. Keep things cordial.
- Ending conversations immediately if aggression recurs. Follow through consistently.

Be open to fully restoring contact once the person can converse calmly and own their behavior.

Sever Ties With Abusers

In abusive relationships, sometimes cutting contact completely is healthiest if the other person refuses to change behavior:

- Make clear the relationship will dissolve without concrete improvement.
- Set firm boundaries around any further contact. Don't get drawn into "closure" talks etc. that turn abusive.
- Ask mutually trusted friends to stop passing information between you. Cut off triangulation.
- Block their number, email, social media so they can't keep contacting you.
- Notify authorities if needed to enforce no contact, get restraining orders etc.

- Surround yourself with loving supporters, not people who undermine your resolve to move on for your well-being.

Though severing ties is painful, it may become necessary. Put your safety first.

Summary

Staying centered in asserting yourself with grace is challenging when met with aggression. But maintaining boundaries while managing your reactions transforms conflict.

Respond to anger with empathy but firmness. Disengage from mistreatment. Resist being manipulated or intimidated into sacrificing your needs.

Handling aggressive responses requires courage and perseverance. But doing so with maturity fosters self-respect and positive change. You model how to have difficult dialogues in healthier ways.

Chapter 29: Maintain Consistency

The key to lasting change is consistency. When learning to be more assertive, it's normal to slip back into passive habits sometimes. Don't let setbacks deter you. Renew your commitment and get back on track.

With regular practice, asserting yourself in healthy ways becomes your new normal. Old people-pleasing patterns lose their grip as confidence grows.

Here we'll explore strategies for maintaining assertive habits long-term until they stick.

Celebrate Small Wins

Notice when you successfully speak up for yourself in ways previously challenging. Appreciate these wins:

- Mentally congratulate yourself after an assertive encounter.
- Journal about the experience and your feelings afterward.
- Tell a supportive friend/mentor about the situation to help reinforce it.
- Treat yourself to a reward connected to the accomplishment.
- Savor the feeling of pride in standing up for your needs.

This self-acknowledgement creates positive reinforcement fueling future assertion.

Revisit Your Motivation

To renew motivation during periods of fatigue or backsliding, revisit why you want to be assertive:

- Reread old journal entries about the costs of passivity on your self-esteem.
- Look at photos illustrating why your relationships matter.
- Talk to friends/family reminded of how assertion helps you.
- Re-watch your favorite movie about finding courage.
- Recall the times you felt proudest advocating for yourself.

Connecting to your core motivation restores commitment when it wavers.

Be Patient With Setbacks

When old habits kick in and you fail to assert yourself, treat it as an inevitable part of the journey - not proof you'll never change.

- Forgive yourself quickly without self-flagellation. Those old patterns were wired in for years. It takes time to form new ones.
- Review what led to the setback and make adjustments, but don't obsess.
- Remind yourself change is a gradual process requiring diligence.
- Recall how far you've come overall. One misstep doesn't erase all progress.

Have self-compassion. Setbacks serve your growth if you get back up.

Identify Warning Signs

Notice the thoughts, feelings and situations that tend to precede you slipping back into passivity. Common patterns include:

- People pleasing thoughts - "They won't approve if I say no." "I don't want to rock the boat."
- Doubting your instincts - "It's not that big a deal." "I'm probably overreacting."
- Wanting to avoid conflict - "Maybe if I just go with the flow, this issue will resolve itself."
- Feeling too tired/drained for a difficult conversation.
- Getting distracted by other priorities.
- Stress causing you to default to old habits.

Knowing your pitfalls allows catching yourself sooner when old patterns resurface.

Have Accountability

Ask assertive friends or mentors to hold you accountable when old habits creep back in. Give them permission to call you out lovingly when you revert to passive old ways.

Their perspective exposes rationalizations you can't see when your thinking gets clouded. External support gets you back on track faster.

Review Your Skills

When passivity kicks in again, refresh your assertion skills through:
- Re-reading previous chapters in this book on techniques to bolster weak areas.
- Re-listening to podcasts/videos on assertion for motivation.
- Practicing scripting out challenging conversations using your skills.
- Booking a therapy refresher session to role play scenarios.

Sharpening your toolbox equips you to keep progressing.

Adjust Your Environment

Look for ways your surroundings may be enabling old passive habits and proactively shift environmental factors in your favor:
- Hang motivating quotes/images related to assertion where you'll see them daily.
- Reduce time with friends who pressure you to stay passive.
- Come early to social events to get comfortable being there assertively.
- Listen to pumped up music on the way to challenging conversations.
- Declutter to minimize everyday frustrations taxing your emotional resources.

Your environment can work for or against you. Mold it to your goals.

Create Implementation Intentions

Write out detailed "if-then" plans to pre-commit to using your new skills when old situations arise. For example:

"If my mother pressures me to visit her when I need a self-care day instead, then I will firmly tell her I can't make it but suggest getting together next weekend."

Having an intention ready for challenging scenarios short-circuits old auto-pilot reactions.

Practice Self-Validation

Counteract thoughts like "I don't matter" or "My needs aren't important enough to inconvenience people" by proactively practicing self-validation.

- Start a daily journal expressing your worth, needs, hopes and strengths.
- Each morning, look in the mirror and repeat affirmations about your value.
- Display notes to yourself expressing compassion for your needs around your home/office.

This daily self-validation cements your worth so it's not as easily shaken.

Reward Progress, Not Perfection

Rather than waiting until you've "mastered" assertion before self-praise, reward yourself for incremental progress:

- Recognize smaller steps like just raising a challenging issue respectfully, even if the full conversation didn't go perfectly.
- Acknowledge effort and willingness to learn as well as specific achievement.
- Maintain progress momentum by celebrating each bit of forward movement.

Small gains add up. Progress, not perfection, is the goal.

Keep Growing Your Comfort Zone

Get into a cycle of continuously expanding your comfort zone instead of remaining in one once you've made some progress:

- Looking back, appreciate how much more you handle with confidence now versus a year ago. Give yourself credit.
- Set new goals that stretch you just beyond your current skill level.
- After achieving that goal, set another slightly advanced one. Repeat.
- This gentle steady growth prevents stagnating. You keep becoming braver.

Regularly raising the bar prevents backsliding.

Learn From Difficult People

Don't just write off challenging relationships as impossible. Consider what trying to assert yourself with them has to teach you:

● Are there strategies you could adjust to communicate more effectively?

● What triggers defensiveness you could better avoid?

● Are there ways to show empathy and common ground even if you disagree?

● What boundaries might be healthy if attempts to understand each other fail?

Difficult people sharpen your skills. Strive to learn from the interactions.

Summary

Sticking to assertive habits requires tenacity when old patterns try to return. But consistency creates change. With self-compassion for setbacks and renewing your skills, determination leads to lasting growth.

Look at obstacles as opportunities to practice, not proof asserting yourself is impossible for you. Small progress sustains motivation better than all-or-nothing thinking.

Keep perspective by comparing yourself now to when you started. Just showing up and staying in motion creates transformation over time. Consistency turns new behaviors into your "new normal."

Chapter 30: Lifelong Growth

Becoming more assertive isn't a one-time transformation - it's a lifelong process. Healthy relationships and fulfilling careers require continually expanding your skills for self-advocacy. Expect ups and downs, but stay committed to your growth.

With regular practice and willingness to learn, assertion becomes an engrained part of who you are over time. The initial discomfort of speaking up fades as confidence builds.

This chapter explores principles for making assertiveness a lifetime endeavor.

Recognize It's a Continuous Journey

Don't fall into the trap of seeing assertiveness as a permanent state you either achieve or don't. Reality involves ongoing effort without an end point.

Like confidence or emotional intelligence, assertiveness must be exercised consistently to sustain it. You're never "done" - it's a lifestyle, not a checklist.

View setbacks or failures not as proof you haven't really changed, but as part of the natural ebb and flow of growth. Keep at it.

Commit to Lifelong Learning

Approach assertiveness with a student mentality, not seeking perfection. Be curious about what works, what doesn't, and how to improve.

Stay open to constructive feedback on your skills. Treat challenging conversations as opportunities to become more effective.

Read books, attend workshops, get coaching to keep honing your abilities. Make learning assertiveness a lifelong endeavor.

Continue Setting New Goals

Avoid complacency by proactively setting new assertiveness goals as you achieve existing ones. Growth requires challenge.

Build on accomplished goals by expanding them. For example:

- After successfully having hard talks with friends, do so with romantic partners.
- Once you advocate well one-on-one, try asserting needs at group meetings.
- After asking for a raise, aim higher next time or request a leadership role. New milestones prevent stagnation. Always have the next horizon in sight.

Diversify Your Skills

Build skills to assert yourself successfully across different personality types and contexts.

For example:

- Learn to stand up to aggressive types without mirroring their energy.
- Advocate with subtle tact in a corporate setting vs. casual ways with friends.
- Tailor your approach for emotional vs. analytical people.
- Develop patience asserting with skeptics yet firmness with manipulators.

Cross-training expands your capabilities since people and contexts vary.

Leverage Your Strengths

While improving weaknesses, also identify and maximize strengths that support your assertiveness:

- Are you naturally empathetic? Use that to have caring, collaborative dialogues.
- Do you easily articulate complex ideas? Use that to explain your perspective.
- Are you confident and charismatic? Project that energy while asserting.
- Are you analytical? Use logic and facts to make your case persuasively.

Great athletes amplify strengths while shoring up weaknesses. Do the same.

When Frustrated, Recall Your Progress

On difficult days when assertiveness feels out of reach, remember how far you've come already. Read old journal entries to see the change.

When you recall past accomplishments, current challenges seem surmountable again. You regain motivation.

Let past wins fuel your self-belief moving forward. Progress often hides behind day-to-day fluctuations.

Accept Imperfection

Striving for perfection with assertion can be self-defeating. People aren't perfect, and conversations won't be either.

Accept occasional awkwardness or stumbles as you learn. Don't beat yourself up over missteps. Stay positive.

Success is getting your needs met while also learning. It's about the overall direction, not isolated incidents.

Remember: Progress, Not Perfection

As mentioned in previous chapters, measuring success via progress rather than perfection is key to sustained growth.

Focus less on each conversation going flawlessly according to some arbitrary standard. Instead, celebrate overall improvement in asserting yourself more often.

Avoid the trap of undervaluing incremental gains because they're not "perfect". Progress compounds.

Maintain Your Motivation

To keep motivated long-term:
- Review your core reasons for becoming assertive whenever you need inspiration.
- Read or watch role models who inspire you.
- Change approaches if they grow stale. Try new self-help books or techniques.
- Surround yourself with supportive people who believe in you, not naysayers.
- Focus on the positive feelings asserting yourself creates when you waver.

Don't let motivation rely on fickle moods. Deliberately nurture it.

Appreciate the Journey

Learn to appreciate the journey, not just the destination. Enjoy growing into a more confident version of yourself.

Savor small "wins" for what they teach you and how they expand your skills, not just anticipating some grand culmination.

Derive satisfaction from giving your best effort and learning from mistakes. You get to choose your mindset.

Handle Criticism Constructively

You'll inevitably face criticism at times when asserting yourself. Don't let it derail your growth.

When criticized:

- Consider thoughtfully if any of it holds truth you should heed.
- Filter out feedback from sources you know come from unhealthy agendas.
- Remember that criticism says more about the critic than you.
- Reframe critiques as perspectives to consider, not objective fact.

Criticism can sharpen your skills if deciphered constructively.

Comparison Destroys Contentment

Avoid undermining your own progress by comparing yourself to those farther along. Everyone is at a different stage.

Stay focused on your own growth trajectory rather than others' paths. Comparison breeds discontentment.

Honor each small step as building your assertiveness skills over time. You'll get where you want to be.

Support Others on Their Journey

Pay your learning forward by supporting others cultivating assertiveness skills too. Be the person you needed earlier in your journey.

You understand their challenges better than anyone. Provide encouragement, share resources, celebrate their wins.

Offer to role play scenarios, attend workshops together, swap book recommendations. Make it a shared path.

Remember Why It Matters to You

On tough days when you're tempted to give up, recall why you wanted to become assertive in the first place. Re-read old journal entries about your reasons.

Remembering your core motivations - improved self-worth and relationships, advocacy for your needs - restores commitment when it wavers.

You started this journey for important reasons. Those "whys" sustain consistency.

Maintain Your Gains

After making major gains, intentionally design ways to cement them as new habits before old ones can encroach again:

● Note which environmental factors support your new assertive habits and amplify those.

● Set reminders to reinforce your new mindsets and ways of communicating.

● Give friends permission to call out backsliding kindly.

Make your gains "stick" through proactive habit design.

Summary

There is no final finish line with developing assertiveness. Expect an ongoing evolutionary process requiring regular practice and renewal.

But committing to assertiveness as a lifelong endeavor gives you the durability to weather setbacks and keep expanding your skills. Progress compounds with consistency.

While the need for learning never ends, enjoy each small step of growth. Have patience with yourself and appreciation for the journey. Your future self will thank you.

Suggested Journal formats

Here are some suggested journal formats to help track your progress in developing greater assertiveness:

Daily Assertion Reflection

Situation - Brief description of a scenario where you did or did not assert yourself.

How I Felt - My emotional state and thoughts before, during and after.

My Response - How I did or didn't advocate for myself.

What I Learned - Insights about my skills, triggers, mindsets etc.

Next Time - What I'd adjust to improve my assertiveness in similar situations.

Weekly Skill Building

My Assertiveness Wins - Times I successfully spoke up for myself.

Areas for Growth - Situations where I struggled to be assertive.

Skills to Practice - What I'll focus on improving next week.

Game Plan - Specific steps I'll take to build those skills.

Monthly Progress Review

3 Big Wins - Major successes in assertiveness this month.

2 Key Learnings - Top insights on my skills, patterns, etc.

1 Game Changer - A new mindset or strategy that made a difference.

Next Milestone - The assertiveness goal I'll target next month.

Quarterly Assessment

Compared to 3 months ago my assertiveness skills are: much improved, moderately improved, slightly improved, no change, worse.

Key factors contributing to progress/regression:

Top priorities to focus on next:

Additional resources needed:

These formats help celebrate wins, get clarity on growth opportunities, and track overall progress over time. Adjust to suit your needs. Consistent journaling builds assertiveness!

Don't miss out!

Visit the website below and you can sign up to receive emails whenever Gaurav Garg publishes a new book. There's no charge and no obligation.

https://books2read.com/r/B-A-TJIX-FHYLC

BOOKS 2 READ

Connecting independent readers to independent writers.

Did you love *No More Mr. Nice Guy*? Then you should read *Harnessing Circadian Rhythms for an Optimal Life*[1] by Gaurav Garg!

[2]

Harnessing Circadian Rhythms for an Optimal Life" is a comprehensive guide that explores the fascinating world of circadian rhythms and how they can be utilized to enhance the quality of life. From understanding the science behind these internal clocks to practical strategies for aligning our routines with them, this book covers a wide range of topics. It delves into the impact of circadian rhythms on sleep, productivity, mental health, aging, travel, shift work, technology, and much more. Readers will discover actionable techniques for optimizing their daily routines, improving physical and cognitive performance, managing stress, and promoting overall well-being. With insights into the latest research and future possibilities, this book empowers individuals to embrace the power of circadian rhythms and unlock their full potential for a healthier, more fulfilling life.

---

1. https://books2read.com/u/47WDpA

2. https://books2read.com/u/47WDpA

Also by Gaurav Garg

One
The Bhagwad Geeta: Ancient Wisdom for Modern Life

Standalone
100 Ayurvedic Herbs for Health and Fitness: Unlocking Nature's Healing Secrets

25 approach frameworks for writing effective Business mails

Ayurveda and Anti-Aging: A Comprehensive Guide to Youthful Living

Navigating Corporate Politics: A Roadmap for Success

The Art of Positivity: Mastering Your Mindset for a Better Life

The Illusion of Perception: How Our Mind Trick Us

Breaking the Darkness: A Journey Through Depression

Analysing Your Dog's Personality: A Roadmap to a Deeper Bond

Karma's Role in Our Conscience: From Angel to Demon and Back Again

Harnessing Circadian Rhythms for an Optimal Life

Mental Mastery: Brain Exercises for Continuous Development

Unlocking the Mind: How Behaviour Reveals Personality

Young Titans: Teach your kids to be mentally strong

Corporate Warriors: Applying Chanakya's Arthashastra In Business

The Don's reckoning

No More Mr. Nice Guy

Milton Keynes UK
Ingram Content Group UK Ltd.
UKHW010654101123
432322UK00007B/466

9 798223 736660